P9-DND-813

FRESH
from the
VALLEY

FRESH FROM THE VALLEY

A Harvest of Recipes from the
Junior League of Yakima

The Junior League of Yakima
5000 West Lincoln Avenue
Yakima, Washington 98908
509-966-0930

Copyright 2003 by
The Junior League of Yakima

ISBN: 0-9721646-0-X
Library of Congress Number: 2002110863

Edited, Designed, and Manufactured by
Favorite Recipes® Press
an imprint of

FRP™

P.O. Box 305142
Nashville, Tennessee 37230
800-358-0560

Book Design: Brad Whitfield & Susan Breining
Art Director: Steve Newman
Project Editor: Ginger Dawson

Manufactured in the United States of America
First Printing: 2003
12,500 copies

All rights reserved. No part of this publication may be reproduced in any form or by any means, electronic or mechanical, including photocopy and information storage and retrieval system, without permission in writing from the Junior League of Yakima.
This cookbook is a collection of favorite recipes, which are not necessarily original recipes.

Pages 38–41 used by permission of
Washington State University Creamery
Pages 155–157 used by permission of
Pear Bureau Northwest
Pages 158–161 used by permission of
Washington State Apple Commission

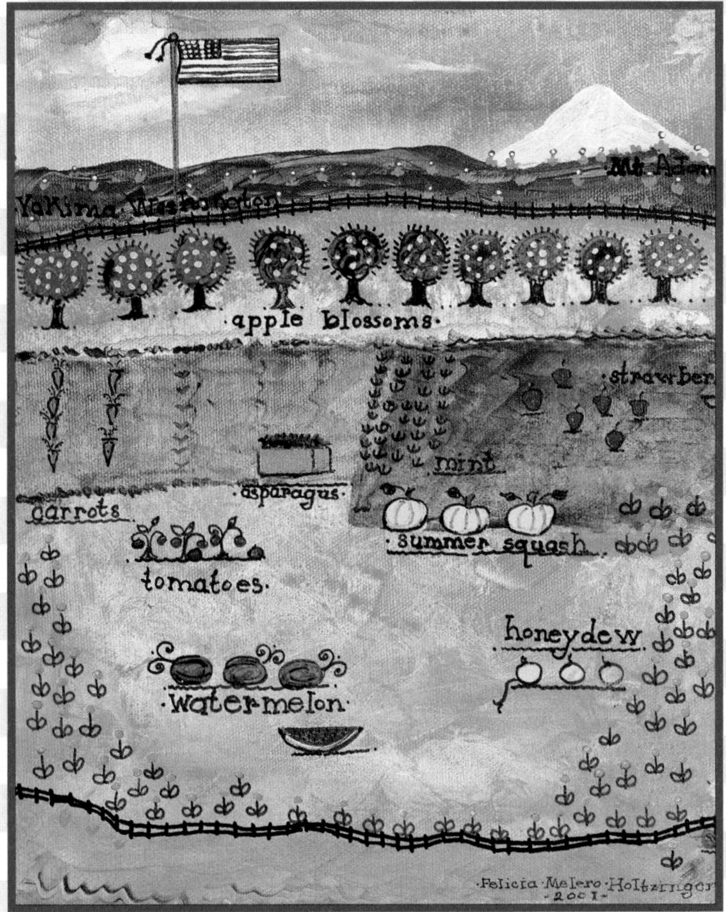

A HARVEST of RECIPES from the JUNIOR LEAGUE OF YAKIMA

THE JUNIOR LEAGUE OF YAKIMA

The Junior League of Yakima is a nonprofit organization of women committed to promoting voluntarism, developing the potential of women, and improving the community through the effective action and leadership of trained volunteers. Its purpose is exclusively educational and charitable.

Proceeds from League fund-raising efforts, including sales of FRESH FROM THE VALLEY, support the purpose and programs of the Junior League of Yakima. A brief summary of how our efforts have benefited the community presently and in the past include:
parent education (Super Storytime Saturday);
literacy (Books for Babies, A Valley Reads);
domestic violence (Domestic Violence Symposium, Domestic Violence Doesn't Work);
immunization (Super Shot Saturday Immunization Clinic);
child care (Yakima Day Nursery);
community scholarships for women; community grants;
and donations to the Capitol Theater, Allied Arts, Children's Village, Sarg Hubbard Park Tot Lot, Millennium Plaza, and Yakima Valley Museum.
Finally, the League provides numerous volunteer hours each year to the community in our community project and Done In A Day events.

The Junior League of Yakima has provided leadership and volunteer service to the Yakima Valley since 1934. We are one of 296 members of The Association of Junior Leagues International Inc., an international association representing Leagues throughout the United States, Canada, Mexico, and Great Britain. The Yakima Junior League is united in a strong and effective network of more than 193,000 women dedicated to voluntarism.

We want to give a special thank you to those in our Valley who provided us with inspiration as well as recipes. The proceeds from the sales of this cookbook will go toward our volunteer efforts and projects in the Yakima Valley. Thank you for supporting our organization.

TABLE OF CONTENTS

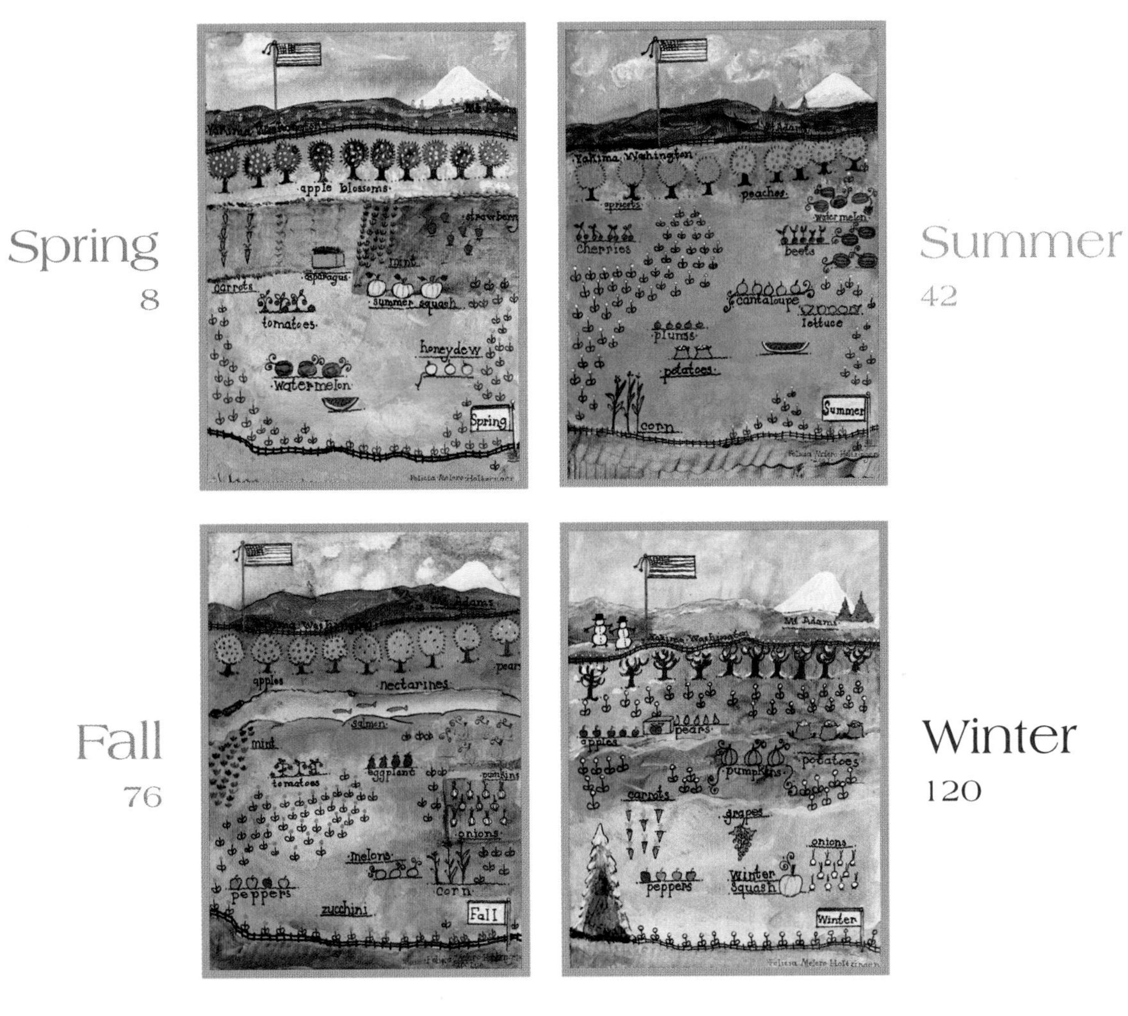

Welcome to our Yakima Valley! Prepare to be tantalized as you experience the wonders of this cookbook. We highlight the freshness of a variety of foods found in our Valley, which is nestled in the center of Washington State. We are surrounded by rivers famous for trout and salmon fishing; apple, cherry, and pear orchards; hops plants, vineyards, and well-known wineries; and fields of peppers, melons, corn, wheat, and mint. The four seasons in Central Washington allow our land to bear many rich tastes. Foods are harvested throughout the spring and summer months, filling our markets with local fare. There are countless people working meticulously and diligently to provide for many others. We are proud of our diverse culture and hope to share it with you in FRESH FROM THE VALLEY. We have captured flavors from our local Mexican influence, as well as rich flavors from the Native American heritage.

Everyone has a favorite meal—something that might spark a memory from the distant past. Remember husking corn on the back porch? Picking berries until your fingers were stained by the sweet juices? The taste of the first juicy, sweet peach just plucked from the tree? Can you smell the peppers roasting on the grill?

The distinct aroma of a batch of homemade salsa? The magical moment when, with your eyes closed, you tasted the sweet crispness of a local gewürztraminer? We want to take you back to those places, help you conjure up those treasured memories, and taste as if for the first time the foods from Yakima Valley. The recipes we are sharing with you came from our families, friends, and first-class restaurants, as well as a few favorites from our NORTHWEST FRESH cookbook. Nestled in this beautiful book, these are recipes that we're sure will become favorites in your home, too. In the tradition of the Junior League, all of our recipes have been tested at least twice to assure that each recipe can be prepared in your kitchen, too.

Our focus in this cookbook is on the four seasons, rejoicing in their great offerings as well as the flavors they bring to the palate. What we have to show you is a mere glimpse of what can be found in this rich, beautiful setting of the Northwest. We want to share some of our favorites with you. Take some time to read about our exceptional ingredients and share your new favorite cookbook with a friend. So, no matter what the season, put on your apron and join us as in experiencing FRESH FROM THE VALLEY.

Spring Beginnings

Blossoms to Asparagus

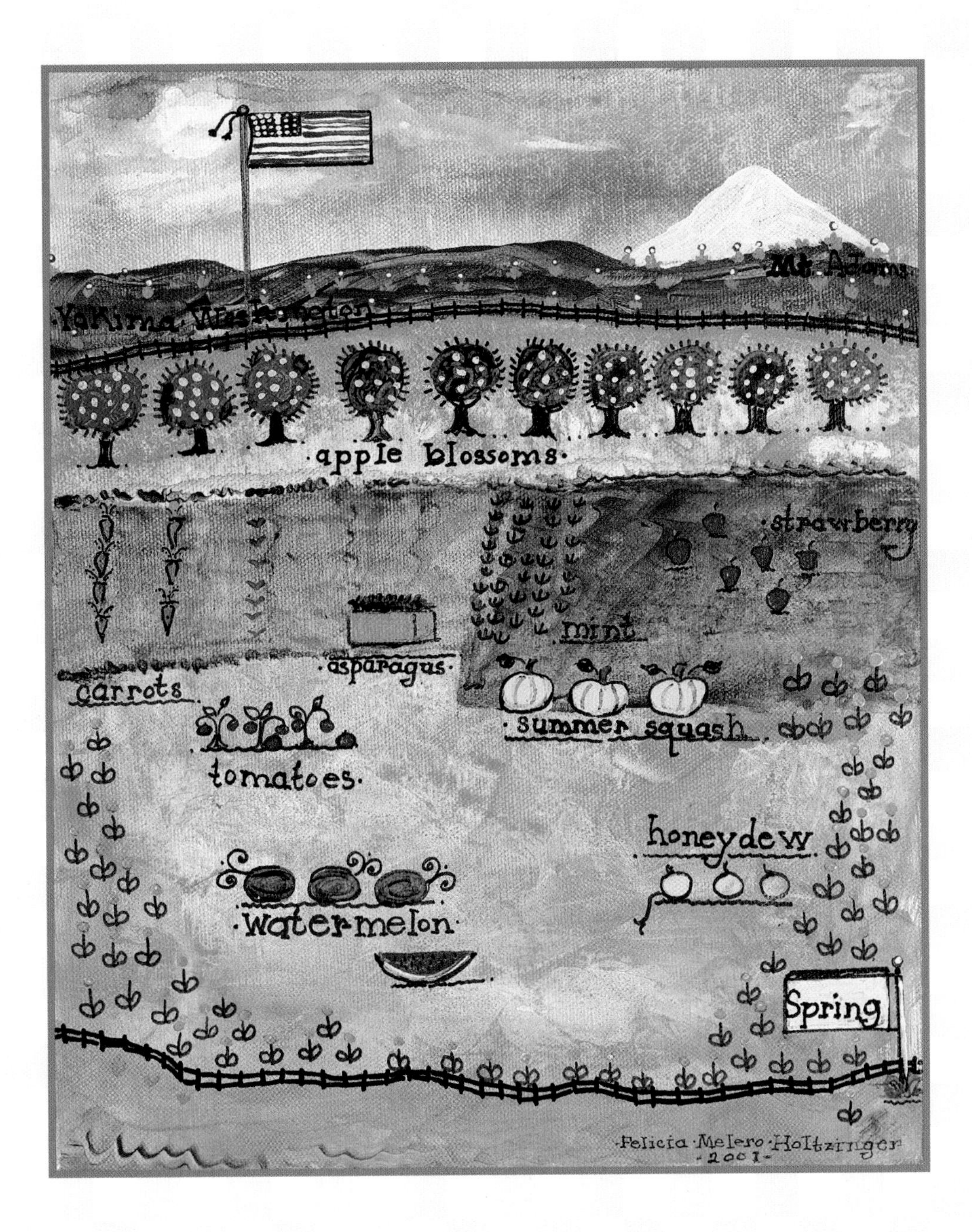
Mt Adams
Yakima Washington
apple blossoms
strawberry
mint
carrots
asparagus
summer squash
tomatoes
honeydew
watermelon
Spring
Felicia Melero Holtzinger
2001

Spring Beginnings

Spring in the Yakima Valley brings the return of cool, sunny days and the celebration of our diverse bounty. The snow begins to melt off the majestic and picturesque Mount Rainier. Daffodils, crocuses, and tulips bring the first yellows, reds, and pinks of the season. The cherry trees start to blossom and the harvest of plump strawberries, asparagus, aromatic basil, and spearmint begins.
Indulge with us and enjoy our Spring.

Bruschetta with Fresh Tomatoes and Basil

Bruschetta is Italian for thickly sliced bread that has been grilled, rubbed with garlic, drizzled with olive oil, and sprinkled with sea salt. This recipe is one of the many variations that exist.

1 French baguette
2 garlic cloves, minced
1/4 cup extra-virgin olive oil
4 very ripe tomatoes, cut into quarters
2 tablespoons chopped fresh basil
Salt and freshly ground pepper to taste

Cut the bread into 1/4- to 1/2-inch slices. Arrange on a baking sheet. Bake at 350 degrees for 12 minutes. Combine the garlic, olive oil, tomatoes, basil, salt and pepper in a food processor and pulse until the mixture is slightly chunky. Remove the bread from the oven and turn. Place a spoonful of the tomato mixture on each slice. Return to the oven. Bake for 5 to 7 minutes or until heated through. Serve warm.

Note: You may sprinkle the bread with shredded Parmesan cheese before adding the tomato mixture.

Serves 8

Pure olive oil is a blend of lower and higher quality olive oils. Extra-virgin olive oil is the richest in aroma and flavor. Green olive oil is pressed from semiripe olives and is slightly sharp in taste, while golden olive oil is pressed from ripe olives and has a delicate flavor.

Torta Rustica

This torta is excellent served hot or cold. Great for picnics.

1 (16-ounce) loaf frozen bread dough, thawed
Frozen or fresh spinach
Sliced onions
Shredded mozzarella cheese, Parmesan cheese or Romano cheese
Fresh basil
Smoked deli ham
Sliced mushrooms
Chopped garlic
Sliced black olives
Salt and pepper to taste
Chopped fresh parsley
Sliced Roma tomatoes
Chopped fresh thyme
Bread crumbs

Divide the dough into 2 equal portions. Stretch 1 portion of the dough in an oiled springform pan to cover the bottom and to form a rim around the edge. Layer the spinach, onions, cheese, basil, ham, mushrooms, garlic, olives, salt, pepper, parsley, tomatoes and thyme in the prepared pan, sprinkling bread crumbs over the layers. Stretch the remaining layer of dough over the top, pressing to the edge to seal. Cover with foil sprayed with nonstick cooking spray.

Bake at 350 degrees for 50 minutes. Uncover and bake for 10 minutes longer or until brown. Let stand for 10 to 15 minutes before serving.

Note: For an open torta, you may eliminate the last layer of dough.

Serves 10 to 12

Black Bean Salsa with Pita Chips

PITA CHIPS

4 (8-inch) rounds pita bread
Salt or seasonings to taste

SALSA

2 (15-ounce) cans black beans, rinsed and drained
1 (15-ounce) can whole kernel corn, drained
2 tomatoes, seeded and chopped
1/2 purple onion, chopped
1 avocado, chopped
2 to 4 tablespoons chopped fresh cilantro
3 tablespoons lime juice
2 tablespoons olive oil
1 tablespoon red wine vinegar
1 1/2 teaspoons salt
1/2 teaspoon pepper

FOR THE PITA CHIPS, cut the pita bread into 8 wedges each. Pull each of the wedges apart to form 2 wedges. Arrange on a baking sheet sprayed with nonstick cooking spray. Coat the wedges lightly with nonstick cooking spray. Season with salt. Bake at 350 degrees for 8 minutes or until golden brown. Let stand until cool.

FOR THE SALSA, combine the black beans, corn, tomatoes, onion, avocado, cilantro, lime juice, olive oil, vinegar, salt and pepper in a large bowl and mix well. Chill, covered, until ready to serve. Serve with the pita chips.

Serves 12 to 15

Fresh Tomato and Sweet Onion Salsa

8 Italian plum tomatoes, chopped
1/2 Walla Walla sweet onion, chopped
1 jalapeño chile, chopped
1/2 teaspoon salt
1/4 to 1/2 cup chopped fresh cilantro
Juice of 1 lime

Combine the tomatoes, onion, jalapeño chile, salt and cilantro in a medium bowl and mix well. Stir in the lime juice. Adjust the seasonings to taste. Chill, covered, for 1 hour before serving.

Note: Omit the jalapeño chile seeds for a milder salsa.

Serves 8 to 10

Fresh Tomato Soup

1 garlic clove, minced
1 onion, chopped
1 rib celery, chopped
1 carrot, chopped
Stock (optional)
1 (28-ounce) can tomatoes, or 3 cups finely chopped tomatoes
2 teaspoons salt
Freshly ground pepper to taste
1 teaspoon sugar
1 teaspoon oregano
1 teaspoon basil
3 cups milk or evaporated milk
1 teaspoon butter, melted
1 1/2 cups cooked rice

Sauté the garlic, onion, celery and carrot in a small amount of stock in a heavy stockpot until tender. Add the tomatoes, salt, pepper, sugar, oregano and basil and mix well. Process 1/2 at a time with the milk and butter in a food processor until blended. Return to the stockpot. Stir in the rice. Cook over low heat until heated through. Ladle into warm bowls. Serve with warm cheese biscuits or cheese broiled on top of fresh French bread.

Serves 6

Chunky Asparagus Chutney

8 ounces Washington asparagus spears
2 tablespoons water
1/4 cup orange marmalade
2 tablespoons minced jalapeño chile
2 tablespoons chopped fresh cilantro
2 tablespoons cider vinegar
1/2 teaspoon garlic salt
3/4 cup coarsely chopped fresh pineapple
1/2 cup coarsely chopped seeded orange sections (about 1 medium orange)

Trim the bottom 1/2 inch from the asparagus spears and discard. Cut the asparagus spears diagonally into thin slices. (You should have about 1 1/4 cups.) Stir-fry the asparagus in the water in a large skillet for 1 to 2 minutes or until the color intensifies. Drain and rinse in cold water to stop the cooking process. Combine the orange marmalade, jalapeño chile, cilantro, vinegar and garlic salt in a medium bowl and stir to mix well. Add the asparagus, pineapple and orange sections and toss gently to coat. Chill, covered, for 30 minutes before serving.

Makes 2 1/2 cups

Asparagus and Walnut Salad

1 1/2 pounds fresh asparagus, trimmed
1 cup walnut halves
1/3 cup soy sauce
1/3 cup sugar
1/3 cup vinegar
3 tablespoons vegetable oil

Steam the asparagus until tender. Cut into 1-inch pieces and keep warm. Spread the walnuts on a baking sheet. Bake at 300 degrees for 20 minutes or until roasted. Chop the walnuts coarsely. Combine the soy sauce, sugar, vinegar and oil in a saucepan. Cook over low heat until the sugar dissolves, stirring constantly. Remove from the heat. Stir in the walnuts. Pour over the asparagus in a bowl and toss lightly. Chill, covered, until ready to serve.

Serves 4

Asparagus in Brown Sugar Butter

3 tablespoons butter or margarine
2 tablespoons brown sugar
2 pounds fresh asparagus, trimmed and cut into 2-inch pieces (about 4 cups)
1 cup chicken broth

Heat the butter and brown sugar in a skillet over medium-high heat until the sugar is dissolved. Add the asparagus. Sauté for 2 minutes. Stir in the broth. Bring to a boil and reduce the heat. Simmer, covered, for 7 minutes or until the asparagus is tender-crisp. Remove the asparagus to a serving dish and keep warm, reserving the sauce in the skillet. Cook the sauce until reduced by 1/2. Pour over the asparagus and serve immediately.

Serves 4 to 6

Dilled Potatoes and Asparagus

2 pounds small red potatoes
1 tablespoon caraway seeds
1 pound fresh asparagus
1 teaspoon sugar
1 teaspoon salt
2 teaspoons dill weed
1/2 teaspoon tarragon
1 tablespoon mustard
1/4 cup vegetable oil
1 green onion, chopped

Boil the red potatoes and caraway seeds in water to cover in a saucepan until tender; drain. Cut the potatoes into bite-size pieces. Trim the asparagus and cut into pieces. Boil the asparagus in water to cover in a saucepan for 7 to 9 minutes or until tender-crisp; drain. Place the red potatoes and asparagus in a serving bowl. Combine the sugar, salt, dill weed, tarragon, mustard and oil in a bowl and mix well. Stir in the green onion. Pour over the vegetables and toss to coat. Serve hot or cold.

Serves 6 to 8

Sesame Asparagus

1 pound fresh asparagus	1 teaspoon sugar
1 1/2 teaspoons sesame oil	2 tablespoons sesame seeds, toasted
1 1/2 teaspoons soy sauce	

Trim the asparagus and cut into 1-inch pieces. Heat the sesame oil in a nonstick skillet over medium heat. Add the asparagus. Stir-fry for 1 1/2 to 2 minutes or until the asparagus begins to soften. Add the soy sauce. Stir-fry for 1 minute. Add the sugar. Stir-fry for 30 seconds. Remove from the heat. Sprinkle with the sesame seeds. Serve immediately.

Serves 4

Toasting nuts brings out their flavor and aroma. Spread whole or chopped nuts or seeds in a single layer on a baking sheet. Bake at 350 degrees for 4 to 5 minutes or until golden brown, shaking the sheet once or twice to brown more evenly. As soon as the nuts begin to brown, they will toast quickly, so watch carefully to prevent burning.

Asparagus with Citrus Sauce

CITRUS SAUCE
1 teaspoon grated orange zest
3 tablespoons fresh orange juice
1/2 teaspoon grated lime zest
1 tablespoon fresh lime juice
1 cup plain yogurt or sour cream
1/8 teaspoon white pepper

ASPARAGUS
2 pounds asparagus, trimmed
Salt to taste

FOR THE SAUCE, combine the orange zest, orange juice, lime zest, lime juice, yogurt and white pepper in a bowl and mix well. Chill, covered, until ready to serve.

FOR THE ASPARAGUS, bring 2 inches of water to a boil in a 12-inch skillet over high heat. Add the asparagus. Season with salt. Cook for 5 to 7 minutes or until tender-crisp. Immerse immediately into ice water in a bowl to stop the cooking process; drain.

TO SERVE, arrange the asparagus on salad plates or a platter. Drizzle with some of the sauce. Spoon the remaining sauce into a serving bowl. Serve with the asparagus.

Serves 8

Arugula with Balsamic Vinaigrette

With a flavor not soon forgotten, this recipe is a perfect accompaniment to any dinner.

8 ounces fresh arugula
2 tablespoons balsamic vinegar
2 tablespoons extra-virgin olive oil
1 garlic clove, crushed
1 teaspoon Dijon mustard
Salt and freshly ground pepper to taste
1/3 cup shredded Parmesan cheese

Rinse the arugula and pat dry. Place in a chilled salad bowl. Mix the balsamic vinegar, olive oil, garlic and Dijon mustard in a bowl until blended. Season with salt and pepper. Pour over the arugula and toss to coat. Sprinkle with the cheese.

Serves 4 to 6

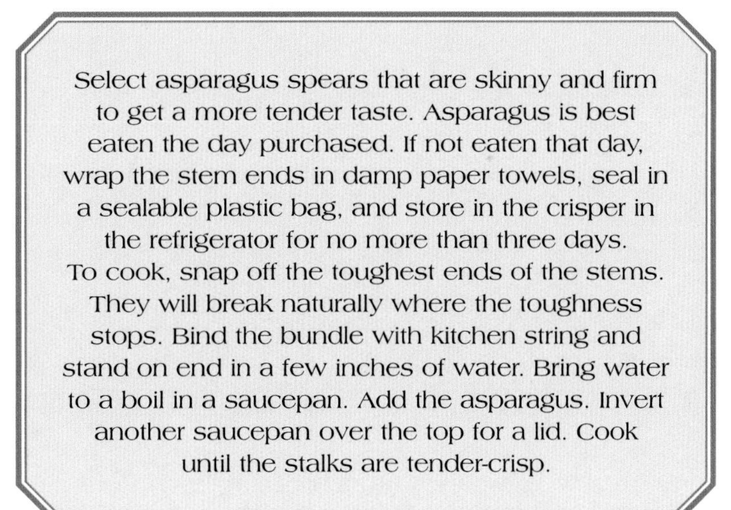

Select asparagus spears that are skinny and firm to get a more tender taste. Asparagus is best eaten the day purchased. If not eaten that day, wrap the stem ends in damp paper towels, seal in a sealable plastic bag, and store in the crisper in the refrigerator for no more than three days. To cook, snap off the toughest ends of the stems. They will break naturally where the toughness stops. Bind the bundle with kitchen string and stand on end in a few inches of water. Bring water to a boil in a saucepan. Add the asparagus. Invert another saucepan over the top for a lid. Cook until the stalks are tender-crisp.

Cannellini and Tomato Salad

1/3 cup orange juice
1 tablespoon extra-virgin olive oil
1 tablespoon white wine vinegar
2 tablespoons chopped fresh basil
2 (15-ounce) cans cannellini beans, rinsed and drained
4 tomatoes, thinly sliced
Salt and pepper to taste

Combine the orange juice, olive oil, vinegar, basil and beans in a bowl and mix well. Arrange the tomatoes on 6 salad plates. Spoon the bean mixture over the tomatoes. Season with salt and pepper. Garnish with sprigs of fresh basil.

Note: To speed tomato ripening, place the tomatoes in a brown paper bag in a dark closet. They will ripen overnight.

Serves 6

Basil brings out the flavor of tomatoes. When using dried basil leaves, crush them with your fingers or mash through a sieve to release the flavor.

Yakima Tomato Pasta Salad

16 ounces bow tie pasta
1 (12-ounce) bottle zesty Italian salad dressing
4 Yakima tomatoes, chopped
1 green bell pepper, chopped
1 Walla Walla onion, chopped
3 tablespoons Johnny's Salad Elegance
3 tablespoons grated Parmesan cheese

Cook the pasta using the package directions; drain. Add the salad dressing, tomatoes, bell pepper, onion, salad seasoning and cheese and toss to mix well. Spoon into a large bowl. Chill, covered, until ready to serve.

Serves 8 to 10

Broccoli-Stuffed Tomatoes

4 tomatoes
2/3 (10-ounce) package frozen chopped broccoli, or 1 broccoli crown, chopped
1/4 cup boiling water
2/3 cup bread crumbs
2/3 cup shredded Cheddar cheese
2/3 cup chopped onion
1/4 cup mayonnaise
1 teaspoon salt

Cut each tomato into 5 wedges to but not through the bottom to form a star shape. Spread the wedges apart. Place the broccoli in the boiling water in a saucepan. Return to a boil. Cook for 2 minutes; drain. Combine the broccoli, bread crumbs, cheese, onion, mayonnaise and salt in a bowl and mix well. Spoon into each tomato and press firmly together. Place on a rack in a baking pan. Bake at 325 degrees for 25 minutes or until heated through.

Note: You may bake in an 8-inch pie plate or ungreased muffin cups to help keep the tomatoes together. You can also use cherry tomatoes for an appetizer.

Serves 4

Fresh Fruit Salad with Honey Dressing

This recipe was handed down from Inez Hardy, a Yakima Valley pioneer from the early 1900s.

HONEY DRESSING

- 2/3 cup sugar
- 1 teaspoon dry mustard
- 1 teaspoon paprika
- 1/4 teaspoon salt
- 1 teaspoon celery seeds
- 1/3 cup honey
- 1 tablespoon lemon juice
- 5 tablespoons vinegar
- 1 teaspoon grated onion
- 1 cup vegetable oil

FRUIT SALAD

- 1 cantaloupe, cut into bite-size pieces
- 1 honeydew melon, cut into bite-size pieces
- Sliced strawberries
- Grape halves
- Sliced kiwifruit
- Orange sections
- Pineapple chunks

FOR THE DRESSING, process the sugar, dry mustard, paprika, salt and celery seeds in a food processor until mixed. Add the honey, lemon juice, vinegar and onion and process until blended. Add the oil in a fine stream, processing constantly until thickened.

FOR THE SALAD, combine the cantaloupe, honeydew melon, strawberries, grape halves, kiwifruit, orange sections and pineapple chunks in a large bowl. Add the dressing and toss to coat.

Serves 12

Ensalada de Margarita

(Fresh Fruit Salad with Pineapple Dressing)

PINEAPPLE DRESSING
1 cup pineapple juice
3 tablespoons fresh lime juice
1/3 cup white tequila
1/2 teaspoon confectioners' sugar
1/2 teaspoon salt
2 tablespoons olive oil

SALAD
1/2 fresh pineapple
2 grapefruit
4 oranges
1 avocado
Lettuce leaves
1 cup sliced almonds, toasted
1 slice watermelon, cut into wedges

FOR THE DRESSING, combine the pineapple juice, lime juice, tequila, confectioners' sugar, salt and olive oil in a jar with a tight-fitting lid. Cover the jar with the lid and shake to mix well. Chill until ready to serve.

FOR THE SALAD, cut the pineapple, grapefruit and oranges into 1-inch pieces. Cut the avocado into 1/2-inch pieces. Combine the fruit and avocado in a bowl. Add the dressing and toss to coat.

TO SERVE, line salad plates with lettuce leaves. Spoon the fruit salad onto the prepared plates. Sprinkle with the almonds. Garnish each with a watermelon wedge.

Serves 6 to 8

Tomato and Fresh Thyme Tart

CRUST
1 1/4 cups flour
1 tablespoon chopped fresh thyme
1/2 teaspoon salt
Freshly ground pepper to taste
1/2 cup (1 stick) butter, cut into pieces
2 teaspoons Dijon mustard
1/4 cup ice water

FILLING
6 tablespoons olive oil
1 onion, cut into halves and slivered
2 yellow bell peppers, seeded and chopped
2 red bell peppers, seeded and chopped
1 tablespoon chopped fresh thyme
1 tablespoon chopped fresh rosemary
Salt and pepper to taste
1/2 cup slivered fresh basil
1/4 cup chopped fresh flat-leaf parsley
4 garlic cloves, minced

ASSEMBLY
1 cup (4 ounces) shredded mozzarella cheese
2 or 3 large Yakima tomatoes, cut into 1/4-inch slices
1/4 teaspoon freshly ground pepper
2 tablespoons chopped fresh thyme
1 tablespoon chopped fresh flat-leaf parsley
1 tablespoon extra-virgin olive oil

For the crust, mix the flour, thyme, salt and pepper in a bowl. Cut in the butter with a pastry blender until crumbly. Stir in the Dijon mustard and enough ice water for the mixture to hold together. Shape the dough into a thick disk. Wrap in plastic wrap. Chill for 1 hour or longer. Roll the dough on a lightly floured surface into a 12-inch circle 1/8 inch thick. Line an 11-inch tart pan with a removable bottom and sides with the dough. Prick the bottom with a fork. Line with foil. Fill with dried beans to use as weights. Bake at 375 degrees for 10 minutes. Remove the beans and foil carefully. Bake for 10 minutes longer. Remove from the oven to cool.

For the filling, heat the olive oil in a large heavy saucepan over medium-low heat. Add the onion, bell peppers, thyme, rosemary, salt and pepper. Cook for 45 minutes or until the vegetables are soft and the mixture is the consistency of marmalade, stirring frequently. Add the basil, parsley and garlic. Cook for 5 minutes, stirring constantly. Adjust the seasonings and drain well.

To assemble, sprinkle the cheese over the crust. Spread the filling over the cheese. Arrange the tomatoes overlapping in a circular pattern to cover the surface. Sprinkle with the pepper, thyme and parsley. Drizzle with the olive oil. Bake at 375 degrees for 40 minutes. Let stand for 10 minutes.

To serve, carefully remove the side of the pan. Run a thin spatula under the crust to loosen from the bottom of the pan and place on a serving platter. Serve hot or at room temperature with a tossed salad.

Serves 6 to 8

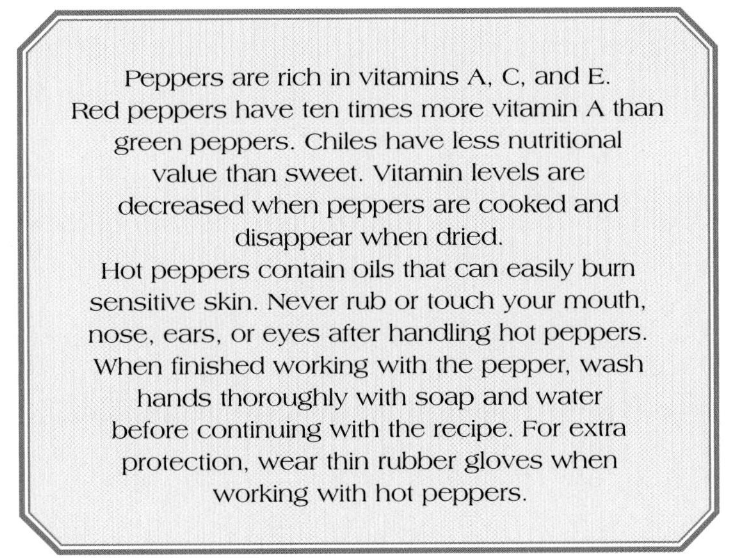
Peppers are rich in vitamins A, C, and E. Red peppers have ten times more vitamin A than green peppers. Chiles have less nutritional value than sweet. Vitamin levels are decreased when peppers are cooked and disappear when dried.
Hot peppers contain oils that can easily burn sensitive skin. Never rub or touch your mouth, nose, ears, or eyes after handling hot peppers. When finished working with the pepper, wash hands thoroughly with soap and water before continuing with the recipe. For extra protection, wear thin rubber gloves when working with hot peppers.

Yakima Tomato Breakfast Strata

1 cup milk
1/2 cup dry white wine
1 loaf dry French bread, cut into slices 1/2 inch thick
8 ounces prosciutto, thinly sliced
8 ounces fontina cheese, thinly sliced
3 Yakima tomatoes, sliced
1/2 cup prepared pesto
5 eggs, beaten
Salt and pepper to taste
1/2 cup heavy cream

Blend the milk and wine in a shallow bowl. Dip the bread slices in the milk mixture and gently squeeze as much liquid as possible from the bread without tearing. Arrange 1/2 of the bread slices slightly overlapping in a greased 12-inch round or oval gratin dish. Layer 1/2 of the prosciutto, 1/2 of the cheese and 1/2 of the tomatoes over the bread.

Spread with 1/2 of the pesto. Repeat the layers with the remaining bread, prosciutto, cheese, tomatoes and pesto. Beat the eggs, salt and pepper in a bowl until frothy. Pour over the layers. Cover with plastic wrap. Chill for 8 to 12 hours. Remove from the refrigerator. Let stand until room temperature. Uncover and drizzle with the cream. Bake at 350 degrees for 45 to 60 minutes or until brown and puffy. Serve immediately.

Serves 6

Fresh Asparagus Pasta

5 garlic cloves, minced
1 teaspoon red pepper flakes
2 or 3 dashes of hot pepper sauce
1/4 cup olive oil
1 tablespoon butter or margarine
1 pound fresh asparagus, cut into 1 1/2-inch pieces
Salt to taste
1/4 teaspoon pepper
1/4 cup shredded Parmesan cheese
8 ounces mostaccioli or elbow macaroni, cooked and drained

Sauté the garlic, red pepper flakes and hot pepper sauce in the olive oil and butter in a skillet for 2 or 3 minutes. Add the asparagus, salt and pepper. Sauté for 8 to 10 minutes or until the asparagus is tender-crisp. Stir in the cheese. Pour over the hot pasta in a serving bowl and toss to coat. Serve immediately.

Note: You may add 2 tablespoons vegetable oil or butter to the hot pasta to keep it from sticking together.

Serves 4 to 6

Yakima Spring Rack of Lamb

- 1/3 cup Yakima Valley red wine (cabernet sauvignon or merlot)
- 2 tablespoons chopped fresh rosemary, or 1 tablespoon dried rosemary
- 2 to 3 tablespoons lemon juice
- 2 garlic cloves, minced
- 1/4 teaspoon freshly ground pepper
- 1/2 teaspoon dry mustard
- 2 tablespoons Worcestershire sauce
- 2 tablespoons olive oil
- Dash of soy sauce
- 1 (8-rib) rack of lamb

Combine the wine, rosemary, lemon juice, garlic, pepper, dry mustard, Worcestershire sauce, olive oil and soy sauce in a bowl and mix well. Place the lamb in a large sealable plastic bag. Pour the wine mixture over the lamb and seal the bag. Marinate in the refrigerator for 8 to 10 hours. Drain the lamb, discarding the marinade. Place the lamb on a grill rack. Grill over hot coals to the desired degree of doneness. Let stand for 10 minutes before serving.

Note: You may place the lamb on a rack in a roasting pan and bake at 350 degrees for 1 hour.

Serves 2

Grilled Mustard Pork Chops with Two-Tomato Salsa

Try this for your next barbecue. It pairs nicely with a crisp green salad and baguette.

TWO-TOMATO SALSA

1 1/2 cups chopped plum or hothouse tomatoes
8 oil-packed sun-dried tomato halves, drained and chopped
1/4 cup chopped fresh basil, or 1 tablespoon dried basil
1/4 teaspoon cumin
1 tablespoon olive oil

PORK CHOPS

2 tablespoons Dijon mustard
1 tablespoon honey
1 teaspoon minced garlic
4 boneless pork chops, cut 3/4 inch thick

FOR THE SALSA, combine the tomatoes, sun-dried tomatoes, basil, cumin and olive oil in a medium bowl and mix well.

FOR THE PORK CHOPS, mix the Dijon mustard, honey and garlic in a small bowl. Rub all over the pork chops. Arrange on a grill rack. Grill, covered with the grill hood, over medium-hot coals for 3 to 4 minutes. Turn the pork chops. Grill for 3 to 4 minutes longer or until the pork chops are cooked through.

Serve the pork chops with the salsa. Garnish with sprigs of fresh basil.

Note: You may marinate the coated pork chops in the refrigerator for 8 to 12 hours.

Serves 4

Spring Chicken and Asparagus

- 1 1/2 pounds fresh asparagus spears, cut into halves
- 4 boneless skinless chicken breasts
- 2 tablespoons vegetable oil
- 1/2 teaspoon salt
- 1/4 teaspoon pepper
- 1 (10-ounce) can cream of chicken soup
- 1/2 cup mayonnaise
- 1 teaspoon lemon juice
- 1/2 teaspoon curry powder
- 1 cup (4 ounces) shredded Cheddar cheese

Cook the asparagus in water to cover in a saucepan until partially cooked, if desired; drain. Arrange the asparagus in a greased 9x9-inch baking dish. Brown the chicken on each side in the oil in a skillet over medium heat. Season with salt and pepper. Arrange the chicken over the asparagus. Mix the soup, mayonnaise, lemon juice and curry powder in a bowl. Pour over the chicken. Bake, covered, at 375 degrees for 40 minutes or until the chicken is tender and the juices run clear. Sprinkle with the cheese. Let stand for 5 minutes before serving.

Serves 4

Dairy products soothe the chile afterburn in the mouth—and this is one time when the more fat the dairy product contains, the better. So if you're going to try some fiery flavors, stay within arm's reach of some milk, yogurt, or ice cream.

Chicken Enchiladas

- 1 1/2 cups flour
- 1/2 cup vegetable oil
- 5 tablespoons chili powder
- 8 cups chicken broth
- 2 chicken bouillon cubes
- Pinch of cumin
- 2 tablespoons minced garlic
- Salt to taste
- 12 corn tortillas
- Vegetable oil for frying
- 1 medium onion, finely chopped
- 16 ounces chicken breasts, cooked and shredded
- 2 cups (8 ounces) shredded Cheddar cheese

Brown the flour in 1/2 cup oil in a skillet, stirring constantly. Stir in the chili powder. Add the chicken broth gradually, stirring constantly. Add the bouillon cubes, cumin, garlic and salt. Fry the tortillas on both sides in hot oil in a skillet. Drain on paper towels, blotting to remove any extra oil. Dip the tortillas 1 at a time in the sauce and place on a plate. Add a small amount of the onion, chicken and cheese and roll up. Arrange in a 9×13-inch baking dish. Repeat with the remaining ingredients. Pour the remaining sauce over the tortillas. Sprinkle with additional cheese to taste. Bake at 350 degrees for 20 minutes or until the cheese melts.

Note: You may substitute browned ground beef for the chicken, or omit the chicken for a vegetarian dish.

Serves 6 to 8

Garlic Chicken in Tomato Cream Sauce

2 teaspoons chopped garlic
1 tablespoon (or more) olive oil
1 tablespoon (or more) butter
Seasoned salt to taste
3/4 cup oil-pack sun-dried tomatoes
6 chicken breasts, chopped
Freshly ground black pepper to taste
1/4 cup marsala
1 (26-ounce) jar marinara sauce
1 tablespoon minced garlic
1 tablespoon basil
1 teaspoon red pepper flakes
1 cup half-and-half
2 tomatoes, chopped
1 (10-ounce) package frozen peas
9 ounces fresh linguini

Sauté 2 teaspoons chopped garlic in the olive oil and butter in a skillet until golden brown. Season with seasoned salt. Remove the garlic to a bowl, reserving the drippings in the skillet. Add the sun-dried tomatoes to the drippings. Sauté until heated through. Remove the sun-dried tomatoes to a bowl, reserving the drippings in the skillet. Add the chicken. Cook until the chicken is brown and the juices run clear, adding additional olive oil and butter if needed. Season with seasoned salt and black pepper. Add the wine. Simmer for 10 minutes. Remove from the heat and keep warm.

Bring the sautéed sun-dried tomatoes, marinara sauce, 1 tablespoon garlic, basil and red pepper flakes to a simmer in a saucepan. Season with seasoned salt and black pepper. Add the half-and-half and tomatoes and mix well. Stir in the peas. Cook until heated through. Cook the pasta in water to cover in a saucepan for 2 to 3 minutes or until al dente; drain. Arrange the pasta on a serving platter. Pour the sauce over the pasta. Arrange the chicken over the top. Sprinkle with the sautéed garlic. Serve with Parmesan cheese and a stout red wine.

Serves 8

Shrimp Cakes with Asparagus and Chive Vinaigrette

CHIVE VINAIGRETTE

1 cup olive oil
2/3 cup chopped fresh chives or green onions
1/4 cup fresh lemon juice
3 tablespoons finely chopped shallots

SHRIMP CAKES

36 fresh asparagus spears
Salt to taste
2 tablespoons unsalted butter
2/3 cup chopped shallots
1 1/2 pounds uncooked medium shrimp, peeled, deveined and finely chopped
1 1/2 cups fresh white bread crumbs
1 cup chopped red bell pepper
2 eggs, beaten
1/4 cup chopped fresh chives or green onions
Pepper to taste
2 tablespoons unsalted butter

FOR THE VINAIGRETTE, whisk the olive oil, chives, lemon juice and shallots in a bowl until blended.

FOR THE SHRIMP CAKES, trim the asparagus and cut into 6-inch pieces. Cook in boiling salted water to cover in a saucepan for 3 minutes or until tender-crisp; drain. Rinse in cold water to stop the cooking process; drain. Chop 4 of the asparagus spears finely, reserving the remaining spears for garnish. Melt 2 tablespoons butter in a small heavy skillet over medium heat. Add the shallots. Sauté for 2 minutes. Combine the shallots, chopped asparagus, shrimp, bread crumbs, bell pepper, eggs and chives in a bowl and mix well. Season generously with salt and pepper. Shape the mixture into 3 1/2- to 4-inch rounds. Melt 2 tablespoons butter in a heavy nonstick skillet over medium heat. Add the shrimp cakes in batches. Cook for 5 minutes per side or until golden brown and cooked through.

TO SERVE, place 1 shrimp cake in the center of each serving plate. Arrange 4 of the reserved asparagus spears around the shrimp cake, overlapping at corners to form a square. Spoon some of the vinaigrette over the top. Serve with the remaining vinaigrette.

Serves 8

Asparagus and Shrimp in Puff Pastry

1 pound fresh asparagus
2 cups mushrooms
2 tablespoons minced onion
1 tablespoon butter
1 tablespoon white wine
Pepper to taste
12 ounces shrimp, cooked
8 ounces cream cheese, softened, sliced
4 sheets puff pastry
1 egg yolk
2 tablespoons milk

Trim the asparagus and cut into 1/2-inch pieces. Sauté the mushrooms and onion in the butter and wine in a skillet until the liquid evaporates. Add the pepper. Remove from the heat. Add the asparagus and shrimp. Spoon into 8 ovenproof ramekins. Layer the cream cheese over the top of each.

Cut the puff pastry into 8 pieces 1/4 inch larger than the top of the ramekins. Moisten the rim of each ramekin. Press the puff pastry to the rim of each and crimp. (You may prepare up to 12 hours ahead up to this point and store in the refrigerator.)

Brush the puff pastry with a mixture of the egg yolk and milk. Pierce the top with a knife in several small places to vent. Arrange the ramekins on a baking sheet. Bake at 425 degrees for 12 to 15 minutes or until the pastry is puffed and golden brown.

Serves 8

Strawberry Devonshire Tart

This original recipe won first prize in the Yakima Herald Republic's recipe contest in 1974.

PASTRY
1 cup flour
1 tablespoon sugar
6 tablespoons butter
1 egg yolk
1 tablespoon ice water

FILLING
3 ounces cream cheese, softened
3 tablespoons sour cream
3 1/2 cups sugar

GLAZE
1 1/2 quarts fresh Washington strawberries
1 cup sugar
3 tablespoons cornstarch
Red food coloring for tinting

For the pastry, process the flour, sugar and butter in a food processor until crumbly. Add the egg yolk and ice water and process until smooth. Chill, covered, for 1 hour. Place the dough between 2 sheets of floured plastic wrap and roll into a circle. Pat into a tart pan and prick the bottom. Bake at 375 degrees for 15 minutes.

For the filling, beat the cream cheese, sour cream and sugar in a mixing bowl until smooth. Spread over the pastry. Chill in the refrigerator.

For the glaze, remove the hulls from the strawberries. Mash enough of the strawberries to measure 1 cup. Force through a sieve to extract the pulp. Add enough water to measure 1 cup. Combine with the sugar and cornstarch in a saucepan. Cook over medium heat until clear and thickened, stirring constantly. Boil for 1 minute, stirring constantly. Remove from the heat and cool slightly. Tint with food coloring.

To assemble, arrange the remaining strawberries over the filling. Pour the glaze over the strawberries. Chill, covered, for 2 hours or longer before serving.

Serves 6 to 8

Spring Strawberry Dessert

1/2 cup (1 stick) butter
1 cup flour
1/4 cup packed brown sugar
2/3 cup chopped walnuts
2 1/2 cups confectioners' sugar
3/4 cup (1 1/2 sticks) butter, softened
2 eggs
2 pints fresh strawberries, sliced
Confectioners' sugar for sprinkling
1 to 2 cups whipped cream, or 8 ounces whipped topping

Melt 1/2 cup butter in a saucepan. Add the flour, brown sugar and walnuts and mix well. Press into a shallow baking pan. Bake at 350 degrees for 20 minutes, stirring frequently. Press 2/3 of the crumb mixture in a 9×13-inch baking dish, reserving the remaining crumb mixture for topping. Beat 2 1/2 cups confectioners' sugar, 3/4 cup butter and the eggs in a mixing bowl until light and fluffy. Press over the cooled crumb mixture with fingers sprayed lightly with nonstick cooking spray.

Arrange the strawberries over the confectioners' sugar mixture. Sprinkle with confectioners' sugar. Spread the whipped cream over the top. Chill, loosely covered with plastic wrap, for 8 to 12 hours. Uncover and sprinkle with the reserved crumb mixture before serving.

Serves 8 to 10

Pavlova

4 egg whites, at room temperature
Pinch of salt
1 cup sugar
1 teaspoon vinegar
1/2 teaspoon vanilla extract
1 (heaping) tablespoon cornstarch
Assorted sliced fruit
2 cups whipping cream, whipped

Beat the egg whites for 2 minutes in a glass or stainless steel mixing bowl. Add a pinch of salt. Beat for 4 minutes or until very stiff peaks form. Add the sugar gradually, beating constantly until very, very stiff peaks form. Beat in the vinegar and vanilla until blended. Sift in the cornstarch gradually and fold in. Rinse an ovenproof serving plate with cold water. Let the plate drip dry. Mold the egg white mixture on the plate forming a well in the center. Place in a 400-degree oven. Reduce the oven temperature to 250 degrees. Bake for 1 1/2 hours. Remove from the oven and cool completely. Fill with fruit. Top with the whipped cream.

Serves 6 to 8

Summer Breeze

8 ounces cream cheese, softened
1/2 cup sour cream
1/2 cup sugar
3 tablespoons amaretto
2 tablespoons whipping cream
1 pint blueberries
1 pint strawberries, cut into quarters

Beat the cream cheese and sour cream in a small mixing bowl at medium speed until smooth. Add the sugar, amaretto and whipping cream and beat until blended. Chill, covered, in the refrigerator. Layer the blueberries and strawberries in parfait glasses. Top with the cream cheese mixture.

Note: You may use any type of berries in this recipe and substitute Grand Mariner or other flavored liqueurs for the amaretto.

Serves 4

Washington State University Creamery

Washington State University has its own Creamery, where students, staff, and visitors may purchase delicious ice cream and cheeses. The cheeses produced have won national and international awards, as well as earned a reputation worthy enough to support a big mail order business. The WSU Creamery is a self-supporting unit of the Department of Food Science and Human Nutrition in the College of Agriculture and Home Economics. Aside from providing jobs for up to fifty students per semester, the revenue from the sales of ice cream and cheese helps support teaching and research.

The Creamery manufactures 340,000 pounds of cheese each year, made from Grade A pasteurized milk produced at the university-owned dairy farm and using lactic acid cultures. Cougar Gold, the most popular cheese, accounts for about 75 percent of the total cheese produced. Other cheeses include a Monterey Jack–type cheese that is called Viking, reduced-fat Viking, American Cheddar, Smoky Cheddar, Dill Garlic, Italian, Black Pepper with Chives, Sweet Basil, and Hot Pepper.

Cougar Gold was the first WSU cheese developed, under the direction of Dr. N.S. Golding. It was a byproduct of research done in the late 1930s to create a cheese that could be stored and shipped in cans. Because most cheeses produce carbon dioxide, a gas that causes the cans to bulge, Cougar Gold was unusual in that it produced very little gas. To this day, all of the cheeses produced here are uniquely packaged in the round cans. Cougar Gold was named one of the "Best Cheeses of 1993" by the American Cheese Society, and was selected tops in its class at an international contest sponsored by the World Cheese Awards in England in October 2000.

Food Finds, a popular show on the Food Network, featured the WSU Creamery and their unique "cheese-in-a-can" in a recent program. Cans of Cougar Gold cheese were taken to Mount Everest by the U.S. expedition in 1985 and 1986. The popular Cheese-Making Short Course has a waiting list for students from the cheese industry and aspiring cheese makers each year.

Visitors to the campus Creamery may taste before they buy. The Creamery also has an observation room with videos detailing the cheese-making process from start to finish. The retail store, named Ferdinand's Ice Cream Shoppe after the animated Disney classic, serves up delicious ice cream cones, milkshakes, and sundaes. You may also book a tour of the Creamery. The Creamery gives tours to over 150 groups a year. THE SPOKESMAN-REVIEW, the largest newspaper in northeast Washington, named the milk shakes at Ferdinand's the "gold standard in shakes" in June 2001.

Orders for cheese—$14 per 30-ounce can plus shipping charges—can be taken by telephone (800-457-5442) Monday through Friday, 8:30 a.m. to 4:30 p.m., by fax (800-572-3289), by mail (WSU Creamery, 101 Food Quality Building, Pullman, WA 99164), or order from the internet at www.wsu.edu/creamery.

COUGAR GOLD

Our most famous and popular cheese
A white, sharp Cheddar with a taste that resembles Swiss or Gouda
Aged for at least one year

AMERICAN CHEDDAR

A sharp, traditional orange Cheddar cheese
Aged for at least one year to develop a smooth, rich flavor

SMOKY CHEDDAR

Natural smoke flavoring added to our American Cheddar
A delicious addition to any party table

VIKING

A mild-flavored, semisoft cheese comparable to Monterey Jack
Aged for at least four months
Great with pasta, in sandwiches, on crackers, or alone

REDUCED-FAT VIKING

Viking cheese with 33 percent less fat; still just as tasty as the original

HOT PEPPER

Just the right amount of jalapeño peppers added to Viking Cheese for a medium flavor that's not too hot; great in omelets

DILL GARLIC

A racy blend of dill weed, dill seed, and milk garlic added to Viking Cheese Terrific with pasta or chicken, but best alone as a snack cheese

SWEET BASIL

Melt-in-your-mouth taste created by seasoning Viking Cheese with flakes of sweet basil; a delightful flavorful cheese

ITALIAN

Zesty combination of basil and oregano added to our Viking Cheese The perfect topping for pizza

CRACKED PEPPER AND CHIVE

Developed to satisfy black pepper fans
Smooth mellow Viking Cheese spiced up with bits of cracked black pepper and flakes of chive

Layered Viking and Tomato Salad

4 large ripe tomatoes, cut into thin slices
2 pounds Viking Cheese, cut into thin slices
1/4 cup chopped fresh basil
1/4 cup chopped fresh parsley
1/2 cup Italian salad dressing
Freshly ground pepper to taste

Layer the tomato slices and cheese slices on a large serving platter, overlapping slightly. Sprinkle the basil and parsley over the top. Drizzle the dressing over the salad and top with pepper.

Serves 6

Open-Face Cougar Cheese Sandwich

1 loaf French, Italian or sourdough bread, cut into 1-inch slices
Bleu cheese salad dressing
Ham slices
Tomato slices
Asparagus spears
Cougar Gold Cheese slices

Spread each slice of bread with the dressing. Layer with ham, tomato and asparagus. Top with cheese slices. Arrange on a baking sheet. Place under the broiler and toast until the cheese is melted.

Serves variable

Cougar Cheese Twists

1 pound puff pastry
4 ounces (1 cup) shredded Viking Cheese

Roll out the puff pastry into a 20x24-inch rectangle. Sprinkle 1/2 of the cheese evenly over the pastry, pressing gently into the pastry.

Fold the pastry in half crosswise and roll out again into a 20x24-inch rectangle. Sprinkle the remaining cheese over the pastry.

Cut the dough into 1/3-inch strips. Twist each strip evenly as for a corkscrew. Arrange the twists on a baking sheet. Bake at 350 degrees for 15 to 20 minutes or until the twists are crispy and golden brown.

Let cool on the baking sheet for 5 minutes. Remove to a wire rack to cool completely. Store in an airtight container.

Makes about 20 twists

Summer Pickings
Cherries to Berries

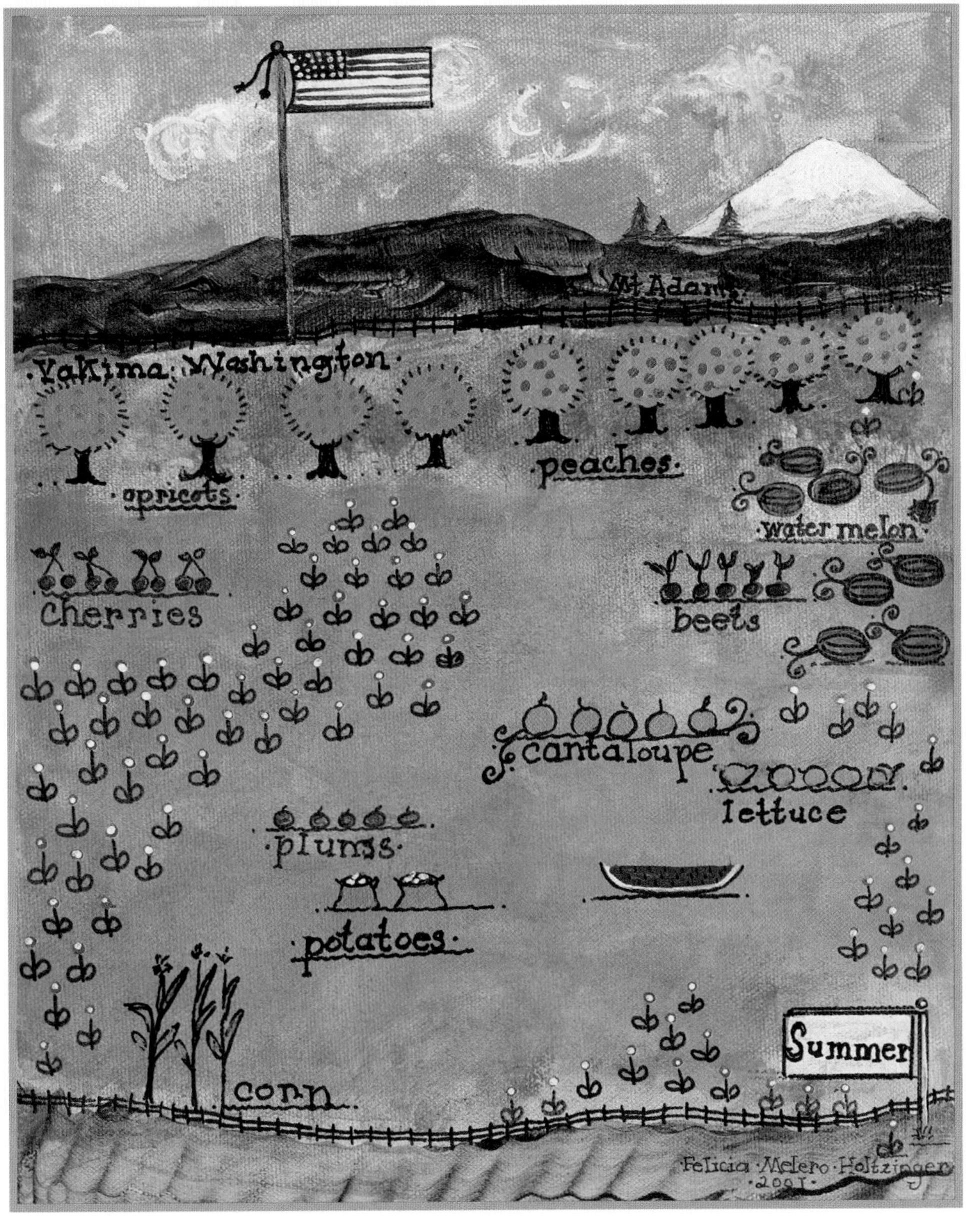

Mt Adams
Yakima Washington
apricots
peaches
water melon
cherries
beets
cantaloupe
lettuce
plums
potatoes
corn
Summer
Felicia Melero Holtzinger
2001

Summer Pickings

Summer days bring growth to the Yakima Valley. You wake to the sputter of sprinklers on the lush, green lawns and gardens. The warmth of the morning kisses your skin as you walk outside to begin your day. The daisies and daylilies are in glorious bloom. The Sunday Market is the place to find sweet cherries, crisp cucumbers, plump peaches, organic lettuce, and much, much more. Come fill up your shopping basket and enjoy the Summer.

Fresh Ginger Iced Tea

For a festive touch, wet the rims of tall glasses and dip in a mixture of finely chopped crystallized ginger and sugar.

1 (3-inch) piece fresh gingerroot, peeled and coarsely grated
4 cups water
1 cup sugar
1/4 cup loose English Breakfast tea leaves
6 cups water

Combine the gingerroot and 4 cups water in a large nonreactive bowl. Let stand, covered, for 48 hours. Line a sieve with cheesecloth and place over a saucepan. Strain the mixture into the saucepan. Stir in the sugar. Bring to a boil over high heat, stirring occasionally. Reduce the heat to medium and simmer for 10 minutes. Remove from the heat and stir in the tea leaves. Let steep, covered, for 5 minutes. Strain into a large pitcher. Pour in 6 cups water and mix well. Chill, covered, until ready to serve. Serve over cracked ice.

Note: For Green Ginger Tea, substitute 12 green tea bags for the loose tea.

Serves 8

Ginger is a very popular herb and spice. Not only does gingerroot add a sweet and spicy zing to a variety of dishes, but the health benefits are numerous. Ginger is a common natural remedy for nausea that is due to morning sickness, motion sickness, and chemotherapy. It is also used to help to detoxify the body because it is a warming herb that promotes sweating. It is excellent in tea or powder form. You can make your own natural ginger ale: prepare a strong tea using fresh gingerroot, squeeze a quarter slice of lemon in the tea and sweeten as desired. Add carbonated water at a 50-50 ratio. Chill until cold.

Artichoke Bruschetta

1 French baguette
1 (6-ounce) jar artichoke hearts, drained and chopped
1/2 cup grated Romano cheese
1/3 cup finely chopped red onion
5 to 6 tablespoons mayonnaise

Slice the baguette into 16 rounds. Combine the artichoke hearts, cheese and red onion in a bowl and mix well. Stir in enough mayonnaise to make of a spreading consistency. Spread the mixture on the baguette rounds. Arrange on a baking sheet. Broil for 2 minutes or until heated through and light brown.

Serves 16

Baked Brie in Puff Pastry

1 frozen puff pastry sheet, thawed
12 ounces or 1/2 small wheel Brie cheese
1/2 cup apricot preserves
1/4 cup toasted pecans (optional)
1 egg yolk
2 tablespoons water

Place the puff pastry sheet on a greased baking sheet. Remove the rind from the Brie and place the Brie in the center of the pastry sheet. Spread the apricot preserves over the Brie. Sprinkle with the pecans. Fold the pastry sheet over the top of the Brie, pinching the edges to seal. Mix the egg yolk and water in a bowl. Brush the egg wash over the pastry. Bake at 350 degrees for 20 minutes or until golden brown. Serve with crackers, sliced apples or sliced pears.

Serves 8 to 10

Spinach and Artichoke Dip in Bread Bowl

1 (10-ounce) package frozen chopped spinach
16 ounces cream cheese, softened
3/4 cup grated Parmesan cheese
1/2 cup sour cream
1/2 cup half-and-half
1/4 cup chicken stock
1 tablespoon hot pepper sauce
1 tablespoon lemon juice
1 tablespoon vinegar
1 teaspoon chopped garlic
1 teaspoon seasoned salt
1 (10-ounce) can artichoke hearts, drained and chopped
1 round bread loaf
1/2 cup sour cream

Cook the spinach using the package directions. Drain the spinach, pressing out the excess moisture. Combine the spinach, cream cheese, Parmesan cheese, 1/2 cup sour cream, half-and-half, chicken stock, hot pepper sauce, lemon juice, vinegar, garlic and seasoned salt in a bowl and mix well. Stir in the artichoke hearts.

Spoon the mixture into a glass baking dish. Bake at 350 degrees for 15 to 18 minutes or until heated through. Cut off the top of the loaf of bread. Hollow out the center, reserving the pieces of bread. Spoon the hot dip into the bread bowl if desired. Top with 1/2 cup sour cream and serve warm with torn bread pieces or tortilla chips.

Makes 5 cups

Mandarin Orange Salad with Cider Vinaigrette

CIDER VINAIGRETTE
1/3 cup sugar
1 teaspoon dry mustard
1 teaspoon salt
1/3 cup cider vinegar
1/4 cup (or less) grated onion
1 teaspoon celery salt
1 cup vegetable oil

SALAD
2 heads chilled romaine, chopped
1 to 2 (11-ounce) cans mandarin oranges, drained
3/4 cup toasted slivered almonds

FOR THE VINAIGRETTE, process the sugar, dry mustard, salt, vinegar, onion and celery salt in a blender. Add the oil in a fine stream, processing constantly at low speed until blended.

FOR THE SALAD, combine the romaine, mandarin oranges and almonds in a large bowl and toss gently. Pour the vinaigrette over the salad and toss gently to combine. Serve immediately.

Note: You may substitute 2 sliced green apples or 2 sliced pears for the mandarin oranges.

Serves 6 to 8

Spinach Strawberry Salad with Honey Mustard Dressing

HONEY MUSTARD DRESSING
2 tablespoons balsamic vinegar
2 tablespoons rice vinegar
4 teaspoons honey
2 teaspoons Dijon mustard
Salt to taste
Pepper to taste

SALAD
8 to 10 cups spinach, rinsed and drained
1 cup sliced strawberries
1 tablespoon sesame seeds, toasted
1 small onion, sliced (optional)

GARNISH
Strawberries

FOR THE DRESSING, whisk the vinegar, honey, Dijon mustard, salt and pepper in a bowl until blended.

FOR THE SALAD, remove the stems from the spinach and tear into a large salad bowl. Add the strawberries, sesame seeds and onion and toss gently. Pour the dressing over the salad and toss gently to combine.

FOR THE GARNISH, thinly slice the strawberries from tip to hull, leaving the hull intact. Fan out the strawberries and arrange over the top of the salad.

Serves 4 to 5

Salad Parmesan

1 garlic clove, minced
1/2 teaspoon salt
1/4 teaspoon pepper
Dash of dry mustard
2 tablespoons grated Parmesan cheese
1/4 cup vegetable oil
1 tablespoon lemon juice
1 head red leaf lettuce, rinsed and drained
1 head romaine, rinsed and drained

Combine the garlic, salt, pepper and dry mustard in a large bowl and mash with a fork until of a paste consistency. Whisk in the cheese, oil and lemon juice. Tear the lettuce into bite-size pieces. Add to the dressing and toss to combine. Serve immediately.

Serves 8

Rigatoni and Cucumber Salad

1 1/2 cups vegetable oil
1 1/4 cups cider vinegar
1 cup sugar
1 garlic clove, minced
2 teaspoons finely chopped fresh parsley
2 teaspoons pepper
16 ounces rigatoni, cooked and drained
2 cucumbers, thinly sliced
2 Walla Walla onions, thinly sliced

Combine the oil, vinegar, sugar, garlic, parsley and pepper in a bowl and mix well. Pour over the pasta in a serving bowl. Add the cucumbers and onions and toss gently to combine. Chill, covered, until ready to serve.

Serves 10 to 12

Marinated Steak Salad

- 3 large red potatoes, peeled and cubed
- 3 cups thinly sliced medium rare beef steak
- 1/3 cup diced red bell pepper
- 1/3 cup diced yellow bell pepper
- 1/3 cup chopped red onion
- 1 scallion top, thinly sliced
- 2/3 cup Italian salad dressing
- 1/3 cup chopped fresh parsley
- 16 ounces mixed lettuce
- Zest of 1 orange

Cook the potatoes in boiling salted water to cover in a saucepan until tender; drain. Combine the potatoes, steak, bell peppers, onion and scallion in a large bowl. Pour the dressing over the steak mixture and toss gently to combine. Add the parsley and toss gently to combine.

Arrange the lettuce leaves on 4 plates. Spoon the steak mixture over the lettuce. Garnish with orange zest. Serve at room temperature.

Note: You may substitute garlic salad dressing or Caesar salad dressing for the Italian salad dressing.

Serves 4

Spinach and Chicken Pasta Salad

DRESSING

1/2 cup vegetable oil
1/4 cup sugar
2 tablespoons white wine vinegar
1 teaspoon lemon juice
2 tablespoons minced fresh parsley
1 teaspoon salt
1/2 teaspoon dried minced onion

SALAD

5 cups chopped cooked chicken
7 ounces fusilli, cooked and drained
2 cups (packed) torn spinach leaves
2 1/2 cups sliced celery
2 cups green grape halves
1 cup snow peas
1/2 large cucumber, sliced
3 green onions with tops, sliced
1 (6-ounce) jar marinated artichoke hearts, drained and quartered
Spinach leaves (optional)
Orange slices (optional)

FOR THE DRESSING, combine the oil, sugar, vinegar, lemon juice, parsley, salt and onion in a bowl, whisking to mix well. Chill, covered, in the refrigerator.

FOR THE SALAD, Combine the chicken, pasta, 2 cups spinach, celery, grapes, snow peas, cucumber, green onions and artichoke hearts in a large bowl and toss to combine. Chill, covered, in the refrigerator.

TO SERVE, pour the dressing over the salad and toss gently to combine. Place a spinach leaf on each plate. Spoon the salad over the spinach leaf. Garnish with orange slices.

Serves 8 to 10

Summertime Turkey Salad

This salad makes a delicious and filling entrée when it is too hot to cook.

1 1/4 pounds turkey breast tenderloins
1/2 cup seasoned rice vinegar
1/2 cup lime juice
2 tablespoons olive oil
1 tablespoon honey
1 tablespoon hot chili oil
1/2 cup minced fresh basil
1/2 cup sliced green onions
1 cantaloupe
1 cucumber, sliced
Salt and pepper to taste
Fresh basil (optional)
Lime wedges (optional)

Place the turkey in a shallow glass bowl. Combine the vinegar, lime juice, olive oil, honey and hot chili oil in a bowl and mix well. Pour 1/2 of the lime mixture over the turkey. Marinate for 15 minutes, turning occasionally. Add 1/2 cup basil and the green onions to the remaining lime mixture. Reserve, covered, until ready to use. Remove the turkey from the marinade and place on a grill rack.

Grill, with the lid closed, over medium heat for 15 to 20 minutes or until cooked through. Cut the turkey and cantaloupe into bite-size pieces. Combine the turkey, cantaloupe and cucumber with the reserved lime mixture in a large bowl and toss gently. Season with salt and pepper. Garnish with basil. Serve with lime wedges.

Serves 4

Turkey and Apricot Salad

1/2 cup lemon juice
1/2 cup vegetable oil
2 tablespoons honey
1 tablespoon Dijon mustard
1 tablespoon poppy seeds
1/2 cup sliced green onions, including tops
1/2 teaspoon grated lemon zest
3/4 cup dried apricot halves
3 to 4 cups chopped cooked turkey
1 Red Delicious apple, thinly sliced
1/2 cup slivered almonds, toasted
Salt to taste
Lettuce

Combine the first 7 ingredients in a glass bowl. Add the apricots and let stand for 30 minutes or longer. Add the turkey and marinate, covered, in the refrigerator for 4 hours or longer. To serve, toss the turkey mixture with the apple and almonds in a bowl. Sprinkle with salt. Serve on a bed of lettuce.

Serves 6

Gruyère Potato Gratin

1 garlic clove
3 large Ellensburg potatoes, peeled and thinly sliced
3/4 cup heavy cream
2 cups (8 ounces) shredded Gruyère cheese
Salt to taste

Cut the garlic clove into halves. Rub the cut side of the garlic over the bottom and side of a 9×9-inch baking dish. Layer the potatoes, cream and cheese 1/2 at a time in the prepared dish. Sprinkle with salt. Bake, covered, at 350 degrees for 45 minutes. Bake, uncovered, for 15 minutes longer or until the top is crisp and golden. You may substitute Washington State University Cougar Gold cheese or Swiss cheese for the Gruyère cheese.

Serves 4

Pesto Orzo with Peas

This is a great side dish for a summer barbeque.

PESTO
4 garlic cloves
3 cups (packed) fresh basil leaves
3/4 cup pine nuts
1 1/2 cups grated Parmesan cheese
2/3 cup olive oil

ORZO
1 cup orzo or rosamarina
1 1/2 cups fresh sweet peas
Salt to taste
Pepper to taste

FOR THE PESTO, combine the garlic, basil, pine nuts and cheese in a food processor and process until minced. Add the olive oil in a fine stream, processing continuously until blended.

FOR THE ORZO, cook the orzo using the package directions in a medium saucepan. Add the peas during the last 4 to 6 minutes of cooking time. Cook for 10 minutes or until the orzo and the peas are tender; drain. Spoon into a serving dish. Add 1/4 cup of the pesto and toss gently to coat. Sprinkle with salt and pepper. Store the remaining pesto in the freezer.

Serves 5

Sun-Dried Tomato Pesto

2 garlic cloves
1/4 cup chopped onion
1/4 cup pine nuts
3/4 cup sun-dried tomatoes
1/4 cup black olives
1 tablespoon red wine vinegar
2 tablespoons olive oil

Mince the garlic, onion and pine nuts in a food processor. Add the remaining ingredients and process to the desired consistency.

Makes 1 1/2 cups

Fettuccini with Pine Nuts and Gorgonzola

3/4 cup pine nuts
1 tablespoon butter
1 tablespoon olive oil
9 ounces fettuccini, cooked and drained
1/2 cup crumbled Gorgonzola cheese
1/2 cup grated Parmesan cheese
2 tablespoons snipped basil

Cook the pine nuts in the butter and olive oil in a skillet over medium heat until toasted, stirring frequently. Combine the toasted pine nuts with the fettuccini, Gorgonzola cheese, Parmesan cheese and basil in a bowl and mix well. Serve immediately.

Serves 6

Penne Vegetable Toss with Chicken

1 garlic bulb
1 cup olive oil
4 boneless chicken breasts, chopped
1/2 pound fresh green beans, cut into 1-inch pieces
2 cups chopped Roma tomatoes
1/2 cup kalamata olives, pitted and quartered
3 tablespoons each chopped fresh basil and oregano
1 pound penne, cooked and drained
Grated Parmesan cheese to taste

Cut the end off of the garlic bulb. Place the garlic cut side down in a baking dish. Pour the olive oil over the garlic. Bake at 375 degrees for 20 to 30 minutes or until the garlic is soft. Let stand until cool. Drain, reserving the garlic and the garlic oil. Sauté the chicken in 2 tablespoons of the reserved garlic oil in a skillet until cooked through. Steam the green beans for 5 minutes or until tender-crisp; drain. Mash the reserved garlic. Add the green beans, garlic, tomatoes, olives, basil and oregano to the chicken. Cook until heated through, stirring occasionally. Toss with the penne; serve with cheese.

Serves 4 to 6

Sirloin Steak with Roasted Corn Salsa

CORN SALSA

3 cups (3 to 5 ears) fresh Yakima corn
4 scallion bulbs, thinly sliced
2 garlic cloves, minced
1 teaspoon kosher salt
1/2 teaspoon cumin
1/2 teaspoon chili powder
1/4 teaspoon pepper
2 tablespoons unsalted butter
2 plum tomatoes, finely chopped
1 to 2 jalapeño chiles, finely chopped, including seeds

STEAK

1/2 teaspoon salt
1 teaspoon cumin
1/2 teaspoon chili powder
1/4 teaspoon pepper
2 pounds (1 1/2-inch-thick) sirloin steak
Lime wedges (optional)

ASSEMBLY

1/4 cup finely chopped fresh cilantro (optional)
4 scallion stems, thinly sliced

For the salsa, heat a large cast-iron skillet over medium-high heat. Spray the heated skillet with nonstick cooking spray. Cook the corn in the skillet for 8 to 10 minutes or until golden brown, stirring occasionally. Remove the cooked corn to a bowl. Cook the scallion bulbs, garlic, salt, cumin, chili powder and pepper in the butter in the skillet over medium heat for 3 to 4 minutes or until the scallions are tender. Remove from the heat and stir in the cooked corn, tomatoes and jalapeño chiles.

For the steak, combine the salt, cumin, chili powder and pepper in a small bowl and mix well. Rub the steak with the seasoning mixture. Grill over hot coals for 9 to 10 minutes per side or to the desired degree of doneness, turning once. Let stand for 5 to 10 minutes before slicing.

To serve, slice the steak. Heat the corn salsa over medium heat. Stir in the cilantro and scallion stems. Spoon the corn salsa over the steak. Serve with lime wedges.

Serves 4 to 6

Grilled Beef Tenderloin with Peppercorn Sauce

PEPPERCORN SAUCE

2 tablespoons unsalted butter
1/4 cup chopped shallots
1/3 cup brandy
1 cup unsalted beef broth
1 cup heavy cream
1 tablespoon peppercorns, crushed
Salt to taste

TENDERLOINS

8 (6-ounce) beef tenderloins
1/4 cup vegetable oil
Salt to taste
Pepper to taste

FOR THE SAUCE, melt the butter in a heavy saucepan over medium heat. Add the shallots and sauté for 8 minutes or until golden. Add the brandy and bring to a boil, stirring occasionally. Add the broth and boil for 5 minutes or until the mixture is reduced to 1 cup, stirring frequently. Stir in the cream and peppercorns. Cook over medium heat for 20 minutes or until thickened, stirring frequently. Sprinkle with salt. You may prepare the sauce 1 day in advance. Chill, covered, until ready to use.

FOR THE TENDERLOINS, brush the beef with the oil. Sprinkle with salt and pepper. Grill over hot coals for 4 minutes per side or to the desired degree of doneness, turning once.

TO SERVE, spoon the warm sauce over the tenderloins.

Note: You may substitute chicken breasts for the tenderloins and chicken broth for the beef broth.

Serves 8

Classic Pot Roast

1 (2 1/2- to 3-pound) chuck roast
2 tablespoons vegetable oil
1 cup dry white wine
1 cup tomato juice
1 tablespoon Worcestershire sauce
1 teaspoon beef bouillon granules
2 teaspoons crushed dried basil
12 new potatoes or Yukon Gold potatoes
8 carrots, cut into 4-inch pieces
6 ribs celery, cut into 1-inch pieces
2 large onions, quartered
1/4 cup flour
1/2 cup cold water

Trim the fat from the roast. Cook the roast in the hot oil in a Dutch oven until brown on all sides. Drain the drippings from the roast. Combine the wine, tomato juice, Worcestershire sauce, bouillon and basil in a bowl and mix well. Pour the wine mixture over the roast. Bring to a boil, stirring occasionally. Reduce the heat and simmer, covered, for 1 hour. Peel a narrow strip from around the center of each potato. Arrange the potatoes, carrots, celery and onions around the roast.

Simmer, covered, for 45 minutes to 1 hour or until the roast and vegetables are tender. Remove the roast and vegetables to a serving platter. Skim the fat from the pan juices. Add water to the pan juices to measure 1 1/2 cups. Combine the flour with 1/2 cup cold water in a small bowl and mix well. Stir into the pan juices. Cook until thickened and bubbly, stirring constantly. Cook 1 minute longer, stirring constantly. Season to taste. You may bake the roast in the oven if desired. Bake, covered, at 325 degrees for 2 hours. Add the vegetables. Bake, covered, for 45 to 60 minutes, or until the roast and vegetables are tender.

Serves 8 to 10

Pork Chops in Balsamic Cherry Sauce

4 boneless pork chops
1/3 cup balsamic vinegar
1 tablespoon butter
Pepper to taste
2 large shallots, thinly sliced, or 2 green onions, thinly sliced
1/3 cup low-sodium chicken broth
1/2 cup dried cherries
Salt to taste

Arrange the pork chops in a shallow glass dish. Pour the vinegar over the pork chops and turn to coat. Let stand for 10 minutes. Melt the butter in a heavy skillet over medium heat. Remove the pork chops to the skillet with a slotted spoon, reserving the marinade. Sprinkle the pork chops with pepper. Sauté for 4 to 5 minutes per side or until brown. Remove the pork chops to a plate. Add the shallots to the skillet. Cook for 2 minutes or until softened, stirring frequently.

Add the broth, cherries and reserved marinade. Bring to a boil, scraping down the browned bits from the side of the skillet. Return the pork chops to the skillet. Simmer for 2 minutes per side or until the pork is cooked through, the cherries are tender and the sauce is slightly reduced. Season with salt and pepper. Serve the pork chops with the cherry sauce.

Serves 4

Chicken with Cranberries

3/4 cup flour
1/2 teaspoon salt
1/4 teaspoon pepper
6 boneless skinless chicken breasts
1/4 cup (1/2 stick) butter
1 cup fresh or frozen cranberries
1 cup water
1/2 cup packed brown sugar
1 tablespoon red wine vinegar
Dash of nutmeg

Combine the flour, salt and pepper in a shallow bowl. Coat the chicken with the flour mixture. Melt the butter in a large skillet. Cook the chicken in the melted butter until brown on both sides. Transfer the chicken to a plate. Combine the cranberries, water, brown sugar, vinegar and nutmeg in the skillet; mix well.

Simmer, covered, for 5 minutes. Add the chicken and simmer, covered, for 20 minutes. Remove the chicken to a serving platter. Cook the sauce until thickened, stirring frequently. Spoon the sauce over the chicken.

Serves 6

Sesame Chicken

- 1/2 cup flour
- 1 1/2 tablespoons garlic pepper or lemon pepper
- 3/4 tablespoon seasoned salt
- 1/2 cup toasted sesame seeds
- 2 cups sliced shiitake mushrooms or button mushrooms
- 1/4 cup finely chopped onion
- 2 teaspoons olive oil
- 1 1/2 cups heavy cream
- 1 tablespoon Dijon mustard
- 1 tablespoon chopped fresh parsley
- 1/3 cup milk
- 6 boneless chicken breasts, chopped
- 1 tablespoon olive oil
- 2 teaspoons dark sesame oil

Combine the flour, garlic pepper and seasoned salt in a shallow bowl and mix well. Reserve 2 tablespoons of the flour mixture. Stir the sesame seeds into the remaining flour mixture. Set aside. Cook the mushrooms and onion in 2 teaspoons olive oil in a medium saucepan until tender, stirring occasionally. Stir in the reserved 2 tablespoons flour mixture. Add the cream. Cook until thickened and bubbly, stirring constantly. Stir in the mustard and parsley; keep warm.

Pour the milk into a shallow bowl. Dip the chicken in the milk, turning to coat. Roll the chicken in the reserved sesame seed mixture. Heat 1 tablespoon olive oil and the sesame oil in a large skillet. Cook the chicken in the hot oil for 6 minutes or until tender and brown, turning once. Transfer the chicken to a serving platter. Pour the mushroom sauce over the chicken. Serve with rice.

Serves 6

MUSHROOMS

The most popular variety is the button mushroom. It has a smooth, round cap and is creamy white to beige in color. The size ranges from small to jumbo. The flavor is mild and earthy when raw and delicate when cooked. These white mushrooms are delicious sautéed in stir-fry dishes or sliced raw and tossed into salads.

The largest and hardiest of cultivated mushrooms is the portobello. Portobellos have flat caps and can range up to 6 inches in diameter. Portobellos are popular grilled whole and served as "mushroom burgers." They are a great vegetarian alternative to the traditional hamburger.

The shiitake mushroom is originally from Asia and at one time grew wild on the shii tree in Japan. It is dark brown, umbrella-shaped, and has a large, floppy cap and a rich, meaty flavor. Use only the caps for broiling, baking, and sautéing, as the stems are extremely tough. Remove the stems from the caps as close to the caps as possible, and use the stems for flavoring stocks and sauces. They are excellent in Asian dishes seasoned with fresh ginger and soy sauce.

Oyster mushrooms are graceful looking mushrooms with caps reminiscent of shells. With their delicate flavor and texture, these mushrooms should not be browned, but rather heated gently in butter or olive oil and served with light sauces and seafood.

Dungeness Crab Cakes with Hollandaise Sauce

HOLLANDAISE SAUCE
1 cup (2 sticks) butter
4 egg yolks
2 tablespoons lemon juice
1/4 teaspoon salt
1/4 teaspoon Tabasco sauce

CRAB CAKES
4 to 5 slices white bread, crusts trimmed and torn
1/3 cup mayonnaise
1 egg, lightly beaten
2 tablespoons each chopped parsley and shallots
2 tablespoons lemon juice
2 teaspoons Dijon mustard
1/4 teaspoon red pepper
1 pound Dungeness crab meat, cleaned
1/4 cup clarified butter
4 tablespoons vegetable oil
8 lemon wedges

FOR THE SAUCE, heat the butter in a small saucepan until very hot but not brown. Combine the egg yolks, lemon juice, salt and Tabasco sauce in a blender and process on low until blended. Remove the cover and add the butter in a fine stream, processing constantly at low speed until all of the butter has been added. Serve immediately or pour into a bowl and place the bowl in a saucepan with 2 inches of hot water until ready to serve. Pour the sauce into a blender and process with 1 tablespoon hot water if the sauce becomes too thick.

FOR THE CRAB CAKES, process the bread in a food processor to make 2 cups bread crumbs. Combine the mayonnaise, egg, parsley, shallots, lemon juice, mustard and red pepper in a bowl and mix well. Add the crab meat and 1 cup of the bread crumbs and mix just until moistened. Shape 1/3 cup of the crab mixture into a 2 1/4-inch patty. Roll in the remaining 1 cup bread crumbs to coat lightly. Place the crab cake on a waxed paper-lined baking sheet. Repeat until all of the crab mixture is used. Heat 1 tablespoon of the clarified butter and 2 tablespoons of the oil in a skillet over medium-high heat. Add 4 crab cakes and cook for 4 minutes on each side or until golden. Transfer to a baking sheet and keep warm. Repeat the procedure with the remaining butter, oil and crab cakes. Serve with the Hollandaise Sauce and lemon wedges.

Serves 8

Shrimp Tacos

3/4 pound (about 24) cooked large shrimp
1/2 cup diced tomato
1/2 cup green salsa
2 tablespoons chopped fresh cilantro
1 1/2 tablespoons olive oil
1 tablespoon fresh lime juice
1/4 teaspoon salt
Pinch of cumin
8 corn tortillas or flour tortillas
2 cups chopped romaine
1/2 cup thinly sliced red onion
Fresh cilantro leaves
Avocado slices
Lime wedges

Combine the shrimp, tomato, salsa, 2 tablespoons cilantro, olive oil, lime juice, salt and cumin in a bowl and mix well. Layer the tortillas between dampened paper towels. Microwave on High for 1 minute. Spoon some of the shrimp mixture onto each of the tortillas. Top with the romaine and onion. Garnish with whole cilantro leaves and avocado slices. Serve with lime wedges.

Serves 4

To prepare shrimp for cooking, peel, starting from the underside of the shrimp. Gently pull the tail to remove. Using a sharp knife, make a shallow cut down the back of the shrimp along the "vein." Pull out the vein while rinsing the shrimp under cold water.

Blueberry Muffins

2 cups flour
1/2 cup sugar
1 tablespoon baking powder
1/2 teaspoon salt
1/2 teaspoon cinnamon
1/2 cup (1 stick) melted butter
1/2 cup milk
2 eggs
1/2 teaspoon vanilla extract
2 cups fresh blueberries
Sugar

Combine the flour, 1/2 cup sugar, baking powder, salt and cinnamon in a bowl. Combine the butter, milk, eggs and vanilla in a bowl and stir until blended. Add the flour mixture and mix well. Stir in the blueberries. Spoon the batter into 12 paper-lined muffin cups. Sprinkle lightly with sugar. Bake at 425 degrees for 15 minutes. Let stand for 15 minutes before removing from the muffin cups.

Makes 12 muffins

For clarified butter, slowly melt unsalted butter in a pan. Remove from the heat and let stand for 2 to 3 minutes, allowing the milk solids to settle to the bottom, leaving the clear liquid on the surface. Skim off any foam that may be on the surface and discard. Strain the clarified butter into a container.

Raspberry Streusel Muffins

PECAN STREUSEL TOPPING

- 1/2 cup chopped pecans
- 1/2 cup packed dark brown sugar
- 1/4 cup unbleached flour
- 1 teaspoon cinnamon
- 1 teaspoon grated lemon zest
- 1 tablespoon melted unsalted butter

LEMON GLAZE

- 1/2 cup confectioners' sugar
- 1 tablespoon fresh lemon juice

RASPBERRY MUFFINS

- 1 1/2 cups unbleached flour
- 1/4 cup sugar
- 1/4 cup packed dark brown sugar
- 2 teaspoons baking powder
- 1 teaspoon cinnamon
- 1/4 teaspoon salt
- 1 egg, slightly beaten
- 1/2 cup (1 stick) butter, melted
- 1/2 cup milk
- 1 1/4 cups fresh raspberries
- 1 teaspoon grated lemon zest

FOR THE TOPPING, combine the pecans, brown sugar, flour, cinnamon and lemon zest in a small bowl and mix well. Add the butter and mix until crumbly.

FOR THE GLAZE, combine the confectioners' sugar and lemon juice in a small bowl and mix well.

FOR THE MUFFINS, sift the flour, sugar, brown sugar, baking powder, cinnamon and salt into a medium bowl. Make a well in the center of the mixture. Add the egg, butter and milk and stir with a wooden spoon just until moistened. Fold in the raspberries and lemon zest. Spoon into 12 paper-lined muffin cups, filling 3/4 full. Sprinkle with the streusel topping. Bake at 350 degrees for 20 to 25 minutes or until firm and brown. Drizzle with the glaze. Serve warm.

Makes 12 muffins

Rhubarb Muffins

MUFFINS

2 1/2 cups flour
1 teaspoon baking soda
1 teaspoon baking powder
1/2 teaspoon salt
1 1/2 cups packed brown sugar
1/2 cup vegetable oil
1 egg
2 teaspoons vanilla extract
1 cup buttermilk
1 1/2 cups chopped rhubarb
1/2 cup walnut halves, chopped

STREUSEL TOPPING

1 tablespoon butter, softened
1/3 cup sugar
1 teaspoon cinnamon

FOR THE MUFFINS, combine the flour, baking soda, baking powder and salt in a bowl. Combine the brown sugar, oil, egg, vanilla and buttermilk in a bowl and mix well. Add the flour mixture and mix well. Stir in the rhubarb and walnuts. Spoon into 20 muffin cups, filling 2/3 full.

FOR THE TOPPING, combine the butter, sugar and cinnamon in a bowl and mix until crumbly. Sprinkle over the muffin batter.

Bake at 375 degrees for 20 to 25 minutes or until a wooden pick inserted in the center comes out clean.

Makes 20 muffins

Peach Upside-Down Gingerbread Cake with Lemon Cream

LEMON CREAM
2 cups heavy cream
1/4 cup sugar
3 egg yolks, lightly beaten
Grated zest of 1 lemon

CAKE
3 tablespoons unsalted butter
1/2 cup packed brown sugar
3 large peaches, peeled and cut into 1/4-inch slices
1/4 cup (1/2 stick) unsalted butter, softened
5 tablespoons brown sugar
1 egg
1/2 cup molasses
1 1/4 cups flour
1/2 teaspoon baking soda
2 teaspoons cinnamon
1 teaspoon nutmeg
1/2 teaspoon cloves
1 teaspoon ginger
1/2 cup buttermilk

For the cream, combine the cream, sugar, egg yolks and lemon zest in a heavy saucepan. Cook over medium heat for 10 minutes or until the mixture thickens and coats the back of a wooden spoon, stirring constantly. Strain the sauce into a bowl. Chill, covered, until serving time.

For the cake, melt 3 tablespoons butter in a 10-inch cast-iron skillet or ovenproof skillet. Remove from the heat and sprinkle 1/2 cup brown sugar over the bottom of the skillet. Arrange the peach slices in a clockwise direction, overlapping them slightly, to cover the bottom of the skillet. Cream 1/4 cup butter and 5 tablespoons brown sugar in a mixing bowl until light and fluffy. Add the egg and molasses and beat until blended. Sift the flour, baking soda, cinnamon, nutmeg, cloves and ginger into a bowl. Add the dry ingredients to the molasses mixture alternately with the buttermilk, blending well after each addition. Pour over the peaches. Bake at 350 degrees for 40 minutes or until a wooden pick inserted near the center comes out clean. Cool for 5 minutes. Invert onto a serving platter. Serve with the Lemon Cream.

Serves 8

Apple Berry Crisp

- 1/4 cup packed brown sugar
- 1/2 teaspoon cinnamon
- 4 Golden Delicious or Rome Beauty apples, peeled, cored and sliced
- 2 cups fresh or frozen blackberries, blueberries, cranberries or raspberries
- 1/3 cup flour
- 1/8 teaspoon salt
- 1/2 cup packed brown sugar
- 1 teaspoon cinnamon
- 5 tablespoons butter
- 1/3 cup quick-cooking oats

Combine 1/4 cup brown sugar and 1/2 teaspoon cinnamon in a bowl. Add the apples and berries and toss to coat. Spoon the apple mixture into a greased 1 1/2- to 2-quart baking dish. Combine the flour, salt, 1/2 cup brown sugar and 1 teaspoon cinnamon in a bowl. Cut in the butter until crumbly. Stir in the oats. Sprinkle over the apple mixture. Bake at 375 degrees for 40 to 45 minutes or until the apples are tender and the topping is crisp and golden. If using cranberries, add 2 tablespoons brown sugar to the mixture. Do not thaw frozen berries.

Serves 8

Waffle Cookies

- 1/2 cup (1 stick) butter
- 3 tablespoons baking cocoa, or 2 ounces chocolate
- 1 cup flour
- 3/4 cup sugar
- 2 eggs, beaten
- 1 teaspoon vanilla extract

Combine the butter and baking cocoa in a saucepan. Heat until blended, stirring frequently. Pour into a bowl. Stir in the flour, sugar, eggs and vanilla and mix well. Drop onto a hot waffle iron. Bake for 4 to 5 minutes or until golden brown. Serve with Homemade Blueberry Ice Cream.

Makes 1 dozen cookies

Homemade Blueberry Ice Cream

2 pints blueberries, mashed
1 1/2 cups sugar
3 tablespoons orange juice
4 cups light cream
1 teaspoon vanilla extract

Combine the blueberries, sugar and orange juice in a 3-quart saucepan. Cook over medium heat until the mixture comes to a boil, stirring occasionally. Reduce the heat and simmer for 5 minutes. Remove from the heat. Purée the mixture in a food processor or blender. Let stand until cool. Pour into a large bowl. Add the cream and vanilla and mix well. Pour into an ice cream freezer. Freeze using manufacturer's directions.

Serves 4 to 6

Marionberry Margeretes

A delicious, buttery treat.

1 cup (2 sticks) butter, softened
3/4 cup packed brown sugar
1 egg
1 teaspoon vanilla extract
1 cup flour
1 teaspoon salt
1/4 teaspoon baking powder
1/8 teaspoon baking soda
1 cup rolled oats
1/2 cup marionberries

Cream the butter and brown sugar in a mixing bowl until light and fluffy. Add the egg and vanilla and mix well. Mix the flour, salt, baking powder and baking soda together. Add to the creamed mixture and mix well. Stir in the oats and marionberries. Spoon into miniature muffin cups. Bake at 375 degrees for 13 to 15 minutes or until a wooden pick inserted in the center comes out clean. You may frost with Cream Cheese Frosting (pages 109 and 151) if desired.

Makes 1 dozen

Cheesecake Supreme with Blueberry Orange Sauce

CRUST
1 cup sifted flour
1/4 cup sugar
1 teaspoon grated lemon zest
1/2 cup (1 stick) butter
1 egg yolk, slightly beaten
1/4 teaspoon vanilla extract

FILLING
40 ounces cream cheese, softened
1/4 teaspoon vanilla extract
3/4 teaspoon grated lemon zest
1 3/4 cups sugar
3 tablespoons flour
1/4 teaspoon salt
4 eggs
2 egg yolks
1/4 cup whipping cream

ASSEMBLY
Blueberry Orange Sauce (page 73)

FOR THE CRUST, combine the flour, sugar and lemon zest in a bowl. Cut in the butter until crumbly. Add the egg yolk and vanilla and beat until blended. Press 1/3 of the mixture over the bottom of a 9-inch springform pan with the side removed. Bake at 400 degrees for 8 minutes or until golden. Let stand until cool. Attach the side of the pan. Press the remaining 2/3 crust mixture on the side of the pan to a height of 1 3/4 inches.

FOR THE FILLING, beat the cream cheese in a mixing bowl until smooth. Add the vanilla and lemon zest and mix well. Combine the sugar, flour and salt. Add to the cream cheese mixture gradually, beating until blended. Add the eggs and egg yolks 1 at a time, beating after each addition. Stir in the whipping cream. Spoon the mixture into the prepared pan. Bake at 450 degrees for 12 minutes. Reduce the heat to 300 degrees. Bake for 55 to 60 minutes or until the edges are golden and the center is set. Let stand for 30 minutes. Loosen the side of the cheesecake with a spatula. Remove the side of the pan. Let stand for 2 hours. Chill, covered, for 2 hours before serving.

TO SERVE, spoon the Blueberry Orange Sauce over the cheesecake.

Serves 12

Blueberry Orange Sauce

1/2 cup sugar
2 tablespoons cornstarch
Dash of salt
1/2 cup fresh orange juice
2 cups blueberries
1 tablespoon lemon juice
2 teaspoons grated orange zest

Combine the sugar, cornstarch and salt in a saucepan. Stir in the orange juice. Add the blueberries and stir gently to mix. Bring the mixture to a boil. Reduce the heat and simmer for 4 to 5 minutes, stirring occasionally. Add the lemon juice and orange zest and mix well. Chill, covered, in the refrigerator.

Amaretto Peach Cheesecake

CRUST
3 tablespoons butter, softened
1/3 cup sugar
1 egg
3/4 cup flour

FILLING
24 ounces cream cheese, softened
3/4 cup sugar
3 tablespoons flour
3 eggs
3 peaches, peeled, sliced and puréed, or 1 (16-ounce) can peaches, drained and puréed
1/4 cup amaretto

For the crust, cream the butter and sugar in a mixing bowl until light and fluffy. Add the egg and mix well. Add the flour and mix well. Press over the bottom of a 9-inch springform pan. Bake at 450 degrees for 10 minutes.

For the filling, combine the cream cheese, sugar and flour in a bowl and mix well. Add the eggs 1 at a time, beating well after each addition. Stir in the peaches and amaretto and mix well. Spoon over the prepared crust. Bake at 450 degrees for 10 minutes. Reduce the heat to 250 degrees. Bake for 65 minutes. Chill, covered, in the refrigerator.

Serves 12

Peach Crème Brûlée

A quick, simple, and delicious mixture of cool peaches, rich cream, and crumbly sugar.

8 peaches, peeled and sliced
2/3 cup sour cream
2/3 cup packed brown sugar, sifted

Arrange the peaches in a baking dish or in individual baking cups. Spoon the sour cream over the peaches. Smooth the sour cream using a spatula. Sprinkle with the brown sugar. Broil 4 to 5 inches from the heat just until the brown sugar is caramelized. You may also use a kitchen torch. Serve immediately.

Serves 8 to 10

Macédoine of Fresh Fruit

1/4 cup rum or orange juice
Juice of 1 lemon
4 oranges, peeled and thinly sliced
2 apples, chopped
2 bananas, sliced
2 pears, chopped
Confectioners' sugar
1 cup fresh raspberries
1/3 cup walnut halves

Combine the rum and lemon juice in a small bowl; mix well. Combine the oranges, apples, bananas and pears in a bowl. Pour the lemon juice mixture over the fruit, tossing to coat well. Marinate, covered, in the refrigerator for several hours.

Layer the fruit in a clear glass bowl, sprinkling confectioners' sugar between each layer to complete four layers. For a variation, do not combine the fruit; layer each type separately.

Top with the raspberries and walnuts immediately before serving.

Note: This is delicious served over pound cake.

Serves 6

Rhubarb Custard Pie

1 cup sugar
1 1/2 tablespoons flour
1/8 teaspoon salt
1 pound rhubarb, cut into 3/4-inch pieces
1 (2-crust) pie pastry
1 (6-ounce) can evaporated milk
3 eggs, slightly beaten
1/2 cup sugar

Combine 1 cup sugar, the flour and salt in a bowl and mix well. Add the rhubarb and toss to coat. Roll 1/2 of the pie pastry into a circle 2 inches larger than the top of a 9-inch pie pan. Fit into a pie plate and trim the edges. Spoon the rhubarb mixture into the prepared pie shell. Combine the milk, eggs and 1/2 cup sugar in a bowl and mix well. Pour over the rhubarb mixture. Cut the remaining pie pastry into strips and weave lattice fashion over the pie. Bake at 450 degrees for 15 minutes. Reduce the heat to 350 degrees. Bake for 25 to 30 minutes or until the crust is golden brown and the filling is bubbly.

Serves 6 to 8

Pie Crust

2 1/2 cups flour
1/2 teaspoon salt
3/4 cup plus 1 1/2 tablespoons unsalted butter, chilled and chopped
5 tablespoons ice water

Combine the flour and salt in a food processor. Add the butter and process for 20 seconds or until crumbly. Add the ice water 1 tablespoon at a time, processing constantly. Knead the dough once or twice. Divide the dough into 2 equal portions. Chill, wrapped in plastic wrap, for 45 minutes. Place 1 portion of the dough at a time on a lightly floured surface. Roll into a circle 2 inches larger than the top of a 9-inch pie pan. Fit into the pie plate and trim the edges. Chill, covered, for 45 minutes. Prick the bottom of the pastry shell using a fork. Bake at 400 degrees for 12 to 15 minutes or until golden brown.

Makes 2 pie crusts

Fall Bounty

Peppers to Pumpkins

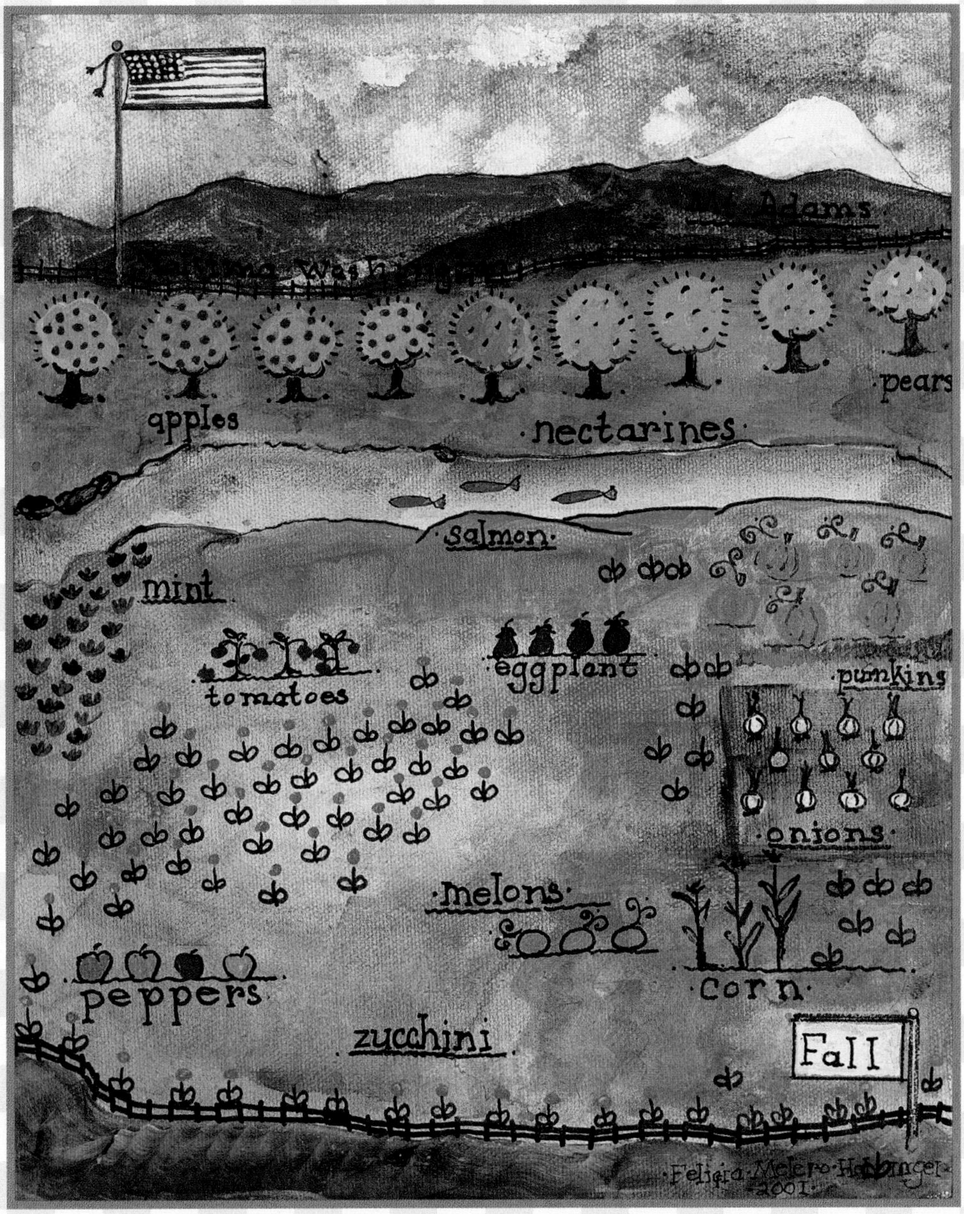
Adams
apples
nectarines
pears
salmon
mint
tomatoes
eggplant
pumkins
onions
melons
peppers
corn
zucchini
Fall
Felicia Melero Holbinger
2001

Fall Bounty

Fall shows us warm days and cool, clear nights.
Vibrant leaves on giant trees change to
wonderful reds, golds, and oranges.
The scent of apples and peppermint is in the air.
School days begin and routines, including homework
and football practice, roll into place.
Crisp red, green, and yellow peppers are harvested
along with pumpkins, melons, and zucchini.
This is a wonderful season in the Yakima Valley—
come enjoy this time and these recipes with us.

Apple Berry Salsa with Cinnamon Chips

SALSA
2 medium Granny Smith apples, peeled and chopped
1 cup sliced strawberries
1 kiwifruit, sliced
Zest of 1 orange
Juice of 1 orange
1 teaspoon lemon juice
2 tablespoons apple jelly
2 tablespoons brown sugar

CINNAMON CHIPS
1 tablespoon sugar
1/2 teaspoon cinnamon
4 flour tortillas

For the salsa, combine the apples, strawberries, kiwifruit, orange zest, orange juice, lemon juice, jelly and brown sugar in a bowl and toss gently to combine. Chill, covered, until ready to serve.

For the cinnamon chips, combine the sugar and cinnamon in a bowl. Sprinkle the tortillas with water. Sprinkle the sugar mixture on the tortillas. Cut each tortilla into 8 wedges. Arrange on a baking sheet. Bake at 350 degrees for 8 to 10 minutes or until brown and crisp.

Serves 16

Smoked Salmon Ball

1 pound smoked salmon
8 ounces cream cheese, softened
1 tablespoon lemon juice
1/2 tablespoon grated lemon zest
2 teaspoons grated onion
1 teaspoon horseradish
1/4 teaspoon liquid smoke
1/4 teaspoon salt
Parsley flakes

Combine the salmon, cream cheese, lemon juice, lemon zest, onion, horseradish, liquid smoke and salt in a bowl and mix well. Chill, covered, for 8 hours. Shape into a ball. Roll in parsley flakes. Chill, covered, until ready to serve. Serve with your favorite crackers.

Serves 20

Garden Patch Dip

8 ounces cream cheese, softened
2 1/2 tablespoons sour cream
2 tablespoons grated horseradish
1/2 cup grated carrots
2 tablespoons grated onion
2 tablespoons grated radishes
1/4 teaspoon salt
3 drops of lemon juice

Combine the cream cheese, sour cream, horseradish, carrots, onion, radishes, salt and lemon juice in a bowl and mix well. Serve with crackers, sliced carrots or sliced red, green and orange bell peppers.

Serves 8

Mexican Appetizer Cheesecake

24 ounces cream cheese, softened
2 teaspoons chicken bouillon granules
1 1/2 teaspoons chili powder
1/2 to 1 teaspoon hot pepper sauce
2 eggs
1/2 cup hot water
1 cup finely chopped chicken
1 (4-ounce) can chopped green chiles, drained
1 cup salsa
1 cup (4 ounces) shredded Cheddar cheese
1 or 2 chopped green onions

Combine the cream cheese, bouillon, chili powder and hot pepper sauce in a mixing bowl and beat until smooth. Add the eggs and hot water and mix well. Stir in the chicken and green chiles. Spoon the mixture into a 9-inch springform pan. Bake at 325 degrees for 30 minutes or until set. Run a knife around the edge of the pan. Remove the side of the pan. Spoon the salsa over the top of the cheesecake. Sprinkle with the Cheddar cheese and green onions. Serve warm or chilled with tortilla chips.

Serves 15

If you are not going to use fresh horseradish immediately, store it in a cold dark area or in a tightly covered jar in the refrigerator or freezer. It will keep for up to six weeks in the refrigerator or up to six months in the freezer. When grating horseradish, wash and peel the root just as you would a potato. And always grate the horseradish in a well-ventilated room as the fumes can be very strong.

Marinated Chicken Wings

1 1/2 pounds chicken wings
1/2 cup frozen orange juice concentrate, thawed
1/4 cup soy sauce
5 drops of Tabasco sauce
1 tablespoon lemon juice
2 tablespoons sugar
1/2 teaspoon minced fresh gingerroot
1/2 teaspoon salt
2 garlic cloves, minced

Place the chicken in a shallow bowl. Combine the orange juice concentrate, soy sauce, Tabasco sauce, lemon juice, sugar, gingerroot, salt and garlic in a bowl; mix well. Pour the mixture over the chicken. Chill, covered, for 1 hour, turning occasionally. Arrange the chicken on a foil-lined baking sheet. Pour the marinade over the chicken. Bake at 350 degrees for 20 minutes, turning once and basting with the marinade. Serve hot or cold.

Serves 8 to 10

Sun-Dried Tomato and Pine Nut Focaccia

Serve this full-flavored dish as an appetizer or an accompaniment to any of your favorite Italian meals.

1/4 cup chopped onion
2 garlic cloves, minced
1 tablespoon olive oil
1/4 cup chopped sun-dried tomatoes
1/4 cup pine nuts
1/2 cup grated Parmesan cheese
1/4 cup mayonnaise
1 focaccia loaf

Sauté the onion and garlic in the olive oil in a skillet for 3 to 5 minutes or until the onion is tender. Add the sun-dried tomatoes, pine nuts, cheese and mayonnaise and mix well. Cook over low heat until the cheese is melted, stirring frequently. Spread the mixture on top of the focaccia. Arrange on a baking sheet. Bake at 375 degrees for 20 minutes or until golden brown. Cool slightly before slicing.

Serves 6

Italian Tortellini Soup

1 pound ground Italian sausage
1/2 cup chopped onion
2 garlic cloves, finely chopped
5 cups beef broth
1 cup tomato sauce
1/2 cup dry red wine
1 pound Roma tomatoes, chopped
4 carrots, sliced
2 small zucchini, sliced
1/2 cup finely chopped green bell pepper
2 tablespoons basil
2 tablespoons oregano
Salt to taste
Pepper to taste
8 ounces cheese tortellini
1/2 cup grated Parmesan cheese or Romano cheese

Brown the sausage, onion and garlic in a skillet, stirring until the sausage is crumbly; drain. Combine the sausage mixture, beef broth, tomato sauce, wine, tomatoes, carrots, zucchini, bell pepper, basil and oregano in a 16-quart stockpot and mix well.

Simmer for 1 hour or until the vegetables are tender. Sprinkle with salt and pepper. Add the tortellini. Cook for 6 to 8 minutes for fresh tortellini or 10 to 12 minutes for frozen tortellini or until done. Ladle into soup bowls. Sprinkle with the cheese. Serve with a warm baguette or your favorite Italian bread.

Serves 8

Roasted Red and Yellow Pepper Soup with Herbed Toast

Worthy of the most special occasions, this elegant soup has a delicate taste sure to put your guests in awe.

CRÈME FRAÎCHE
1/2 cup whipping cream
1 tablespoon buttermilk

HERBED TOAST
1 baguette, cut into 1/2-inch slices
6 tablespoons chopped fresh parsley
3 tablespoons chopped fresh basil
3 tablespoons extra-virgin olive oil
Salt to taste
Freshly ground pepper to taste

SOUP
1 large yellow onion, chopped
2 large shallots, chopped
2 garlic cloves, chopped
2 tablespoons extra-virgin olive oil
3/4 cup dry sherry
1 quart chicken broth
1 bay leaf
3 sprigs of thyme
2 sprigs of parsley
Freshly ground pepper to taste
4 roasted red bell peppers, peeled, seeded and chopped
4 roasted yellow bell peppers, peeled, seeded and chopped

For the crème fraîche, combine the whipping cream and buttermilk in a jar with a tight-fitting lid. Let stand at room temperature for 8 to 24 hours or until very thick. You may store the crème fraîche, covered, in the refrigerator for up to 10 days.

For the herbed toast, arrange the baguette slices on a baking sheet. Bake at 400 degrees for 10 minutes or until light brown. Combine the parsley, basil, olive oil, salt and pepper in a bowl and mix well. Spread over the toasted baguette slices.

For the soup, sauté the onion, shallots and garlic in the olive oil in a large saucepan. Stir in the sherry. Cook for 10 minutes or until the liquid evaporates, stirring frequently. Add the chicken broth, bay leaf, thyme, parsley and pepper and mix well.

Cook for 10 minutes, stirring occasionally. Remove the bay leaf, the sprigs of thyme and sprigs of parsley. Combine 1/2 of the sherry mixture with the red bell peppers in a blender and process until smooth. Pour into a saucepan. Repeat the process with the yellow bell peppers and remaining sherry mixture. Pour into a separate saucepan.

You may prepare the soup up to this point and chill, covered, for 24 hours or until ready to serve. Heat both saucepans of soup over low heat. Pour each mixture into a spouted pitcher. Pour the soups into soup bowls at the same time. Top each with a dollop of crème fraîche and serve with the herbed toast.

Serves 6

To roast bell peppers, arrange the peppers on a baking sheet. Broil until the skins blister and turn black. Transfer the peppers to a sealable plastic bag and tightly seal the end. Let stand to steam.

Autumn Harvest Soup

1 ($6^{1}/_{2}$- to 9-pound) pumpkin
6 to 7 cups croutons
1 cup (4 ounces) shredded Gruyère cheese
Salt to taste
Pepper to taste
3 quarts light cream

Cut a lid from the top of the pumpkin by cutting around the stem. Remove and discard the seeds and fibers being careful to leave the pumpkin pulp. Alternate layers of croutons and cheese in the pumpkin until all of the ingredients are used. Season with salt and pepper. Pour the cream over the prepared layers. Cover tightly with the pumpkin lid. Place on a baking sheet. Bake at 350 degrees for 2 hours. Remove the lid. Stir gently to combine, incorporating the flesh from the pumpkin. The soup should be thick. Ladle from the pumpkin into soup bowls.

Serves 6 to 8

Cinnamon-Spiced Pumpkin Soup

1 (15-ounce) can pumpkin
1 (14-ounce) can chicken broth
1 cup milk
1 tablespoon brown sugar
$^{1}/_{4}$ teaspoon cinnamon
$^{1}/_{2}$ to $^{1}/_{4}$ teaspoon nutmeg
$^{1}/_{4}$ teaspoon salt (optional)
Chopped chives (optional)

Combine the pumpkin, chicken broth and milk in a large saucepan. Stir in the brown sugar, cinnamon, nutmeg and salt. Bring to a boil, stirring occasionally. Reduce the heat and simmer, uncovered, for 5 minutes, stirring occasionally. Ladle into soup bowls. Sprinkle with chives. Serve warm or chilled.

Note: You may substitute $^{1}/_{2}$ tablespoon curry powder for the cinnamon if desired.

Serves 6

THE HISTORY OF PUMPKINS

Pumpkins are believed to have originated in Central America. Seeds from related plants have been found in Mexico dating back over 7000 years to 5500 B.C. Native Americans used pumpkins as a staple in their diets centuries before the pilgrims landed. When white settlers arrived, they saw the pumpkins grown by the indians and the fruit soon became a staple in their diet as well. They brought seeds to Europe where pumpkins quickly became popular. Early settlers used pumpkins for recipes from desserts to stews, as we do today. In addition to cooking, they also dried pumpkin shells and cut strips to weave into mats. Early settlers made pumpkin pie by filling a hollowed-out pumpkin shell with milk, honey, and spices, then baking it.

Pumpkin carving is a popular part of modern America's Halloween celebration. Come October, pumpkins can be found everywhere in this country from front porches to dinner tables.

For centuries, people have been making jack-o'-lanterns by carving scary faces into turnips, potatoes, or large beets and placing them in windows to frighten away evil spirits. Irish and Scotch immigrants brought the jack-o'-lantern tradition with them when they came to the United States. They soon found that pumpkins, a fruit native to America, made the perfect jack-o'-lantern.

Chinese Apple Salad with Soy Dressing

This light, refreshing salad makes a delicious side dish
for grilled meats and chicken.

SOY DRESSING
3 tablespoons vegetable oil
2 tablespoons cider vinegar
1 tablespoon soy sauce
1/4 teaspoon black pepper

SALAD
1 Granny Smith apple, chopped
1 cup sliced mushrooms
1 cup bean sprouts
1 cup snow pea pods
1/4 cup sliced celery
1/4 cup chopped green bell pepper

FOR THE DRESSING, combine the oil, vinegar, soy sauce and pepper in a bowl and whisk until blended.

FOR THE SALAD, combine the apple, mushrooms, bean sprouts, pea pods, celery and bell pepper in a bowl and toss to combine. Pour the dressing over the salad and toss gently to coat.

Note: You may add chopped cooked chicken, fish or pork for a main dish salad.

Serves 6

Use your egg slicer to make slicing mushrooms easier. The egg slicer makes even slices and saves time.

Apple and Wilted Lettuce Salad with Hot Bacon Dressing

6 cups torn romaine
4 cups torn green or red leaf lettuce
2 Red Delicious or Golden Delicious apples, chopped
1/2 cup chopped celery
6 slices bacon
1/3 cup cider vinegar
1/4 cup water
1 envelope Italian salad dressing mix
2 teaspoons sugar
1/4 cup sliced green onions
Pepper to taste

Combine the lettuce, apples and celery in a large bowl and toss to mix. Fry the bacon in a skillet until crisp. Drain, reserving the drippings. Crumble the bacon and sprinkle over the salad. Combine the reserved bacon drippings, vinegar, water, salad dressing mix and sugar in a saucepan. Bring to a boil, stirring frequently. Pour over the salad. Sprinkle with the green onions and pepper. Serve immediately.

Serves 6

Harvest Apple Slaw

The crunchiness and sweet tastes in this unique salad combine for a magical mix.

DRESSING
2 cups mayonnaise
1/2 cup rice vinegar
1/2 cup sugar

SLAW
1 head cabbage, chopped
1 Gala apple or Fuji apple, chopped
1 Granny Smith apple, chopped
1 Bartlett pear or Anjou pear, chopped
4 large or 8 small garlic cloves, finely chopped
1 tablespoon butter
1 tablespoon olive oil
3/4 teaspoon seasoned salt
1 cup pine nuts
1 cup dried cranberries

FOR THE DRESSING, combine the mayonnaise, vinegar and sugar in a bowl and mix with a wooden spoon.

FOR THE SLAW, combine the cabbage, apples and pear in a large bowl and toss to mix. Sauté the garlic in the butter and olive oil in a skillet over medium heat until the garlic is golden and crisp. Do not burn. Remove the garlic from the pan, reserving the butter and olive oil. Add the seasoned salt. Sauté the pine nuts in the reserved butter and olive oil in a skillet over medium-high heat until golden. Add the garlic, pine nuts and cranberries to the cabbage mixture and toss to combine. Add the dressing and toss to coat.

Note: Do not use craisins, which are sweetened and have a red dye that will color your dressing.

Serves 8 to 10

Lemon Zucchini Salad

4 to 5 tablespoons extra-virgin olive oil
3 to 4 tablespoons fresh lemon juice
Salt to taste
Freshly ground black pepper to taste
4 zucchini, coarsely chopped
1/4 cup grated Parmesan cheese

Combine the olive oil, lemon juice, salt and pepper in a bowl and whisk until blended. Add the zucchini and cheese and toss gently to combine. Chill, covered, until ready to serve.

Serves 8

Zucchini and Tomato with Parmesan

6 small zucchini, sliced
1 rib celery, chopped
1 onion, chopped
1 tablespoon marjoram
1 tablespoon oregano
1 teaspoon salt
1/4 teaspoon pepper
2 tablespoons butter
1 (8-ounce) can tomato sauce
1 tomato, sliced
1/2 cup grated Parmesan cheese

Cook the zucchini, celery, onion, marjoram, oregano, salt and pepper in the butter in a large skillet over medium-high heat until the vegetables are tender-crisp, stirring frequently. Reduce the heat. Pour the tomato sauce over the vegetables. Arrange the tomato slices over the top of the vegetables. Sprinkle with the cheese. Simmer, covered, for 35 to 45 minutes or until the vegetables are tender.

Serves 6

Grilled Vegetables

1/2 cup olive oil
2 tablespoons balsamic vinegar
1 teaspoon oregano
Salt to taste
Pepper to taste
3 eggplant, sliced into halves lengthwise
3 red bell peppers, sliced into halves lengthwise and seeded
3 zucchini, sliced into halves lengthwise
1 large red onion, sliced in 1/4-inch slices
1/2 cup olive oil
1 cup (4 ounces) shredded mozzarella cheese

Whisk 1/2 cup olive oil, the balsamic vinegar, oregano, salt and pepper in a bowl. Grill the eggplant, bell peppers, zucchini and onion over hot coals until cooked through but still firm, basting with 1/2 cup olive oil. The eggplant should take about 8 minutes to cook, the bell peppers about 8 to 10 minutes and the zucchini about 5 to 6 minutes. Cut the vegetables into strips and remove to a large bowl. Pour the vinegar mixture over the vegetables and toss to coat. Serve with the cheese.

Serves 6

At the grocery, choose an eggplant that is firm and heavy with tight skin. Feel for a bit of a yield when applying pressure to eggplant. If it is too soft, the eggplant will be bitter; if too hard, it is not ripe.
Eggplant will keep for 4 to 5 days. It is best stored in a plastic bag in the refrigerator.
Salting eggplant prior to frying or any quick-cooking method prevents it from being mushy and tasting bitter. To salt an eggplant, cut it as directed by the recipe and spread the pieces on paper towels. Sprinkle with salt.

Indian Summer Frittata

1 cup sliced frozen artichoke hearts, thawed and drained
1 cup chopped zucchini
2/3 cup chopped onion
2/3 cup chopped red bell pepper or green bell pepper
1 teaspoon minced garlic
2 tablespoons vegetable oil
5 eggs
1/3 cup milk
1/2 teaspoon salt
Dash of pepper
1 1/2 cups soft bread cubes
1 cup (4 ounces) shredded Cheddar cheese
8 ounces cream cheese, cubed

Sauté the artichoke hearts, zucchini, onion, bell pepper and garlic in the oil in a skillet until tender-crisp. Combine the eggs, milk, salt and pepper in a bowl and beat until blended. Add the vegetable mixture, bread cubes, Cheddar cheese and cream cheese and toss gently to combine. Spoon into a greased 9-inch pie plate. Bake at 350 degrees for 45 minutes or until light brown and set. Cool for 5 to 10 minutes before slicing.

Note: You may also prepare this dish with fresh artichokes.

Serves 6

When purchasing artichokes, select those that are soft green in color with tightly packed leaves. Artichokes will keep longer if sprinkled with a few drops of water before sealing in a plastic bag. Store in the refrigerator until ready to use. To prepare artichokes for cooking, rinse under running water. Remove the lower outer petals. Cut the tips off the petals, and trim the stems to an inch or less. Boil or steam artichokes by standing the artichokes in 3 quarts boiling salted water in a large saucepan. Boil gently, covered, for 20 to 40 minutes or until a petal near the center pulls out easily.

Zucchini and Tomato Frittata

8 eggs, beaten
1/4 cup grated Parmesan
cheese
2 tablespoons minced chives
or green onions
1/2 teaspoon salt
1/4 teaspoon pepper
2 zucchini, thinly sliced
1 tablespoon extra-virgin
olive oil
1/4 cup thinly sliced Walla
Walla onion
1 tomato, peeled and
chopped
1 garlic clove, minced
1 tablespoon extra-virgin
olive oil

Whisk the eggs, cheese, chives, salt and pepper in a bowl. Cook 1 of the zucchini in 1 tablespoon hot olive oil in an ovenproof skillet for 3 minutes or until tender, stirring frequently. Transfer to a small bowl. Repeat the procedure with the remaining zucchini. Cook the onion, tomato and garlic in 1 tablespoon olive oil in the same skillet for 5 minutes or until the garlic is tender, stirring frequently. Stir in the cooked zucchini. Pour in the egg mixture. Cook for 3 minutes or just until the bottom of the frittata is set. Bake the frittata at 350 degrees for 12 to 15 minutes or until golden brown and completely set. Invert onto a serving plate.

Serves 8

After rinsing your tomato, try one of the following methods to easily peel. Stroke the peel with the dull edge of a knife blade until the peel wrinkles and can be lifted off. Immerse the tomato in boiling water for 1 minute then immediately immerse in cold water. Drain and peel. Pierce the tomato with a fork and rotate over a hot stovetop burner until the peel is tight and shiny. Plunge into cold water and peel.

Apple Pancake

2 apples, peeled and chopped
2 tablespoons lemon juice
2 tablespoons sugar
1/2 teaspoon cinnamon
2 tablespoons butter
3 eggs
1/2 cup milk
2 tablespoons melted butter
1/2 cup flour
1/2 teaspoon salt
1 tablespoon confectioners' sugar

Toss the apples with the lemon juice in a bowl. Combine the sugar and cinnamon and sprinkle over the apples. Cook the apple mixture in 2 tablespoons butter in an ovenproof skillet until tender, stirring frequently. Combine the eggs, milk, 2 tablespoons melted butter, flour and salt in a bowl and whisk until blended. Pour the egg mixture over the apples. Bake at 425 degrees for 15 to 20 minutes or until golden and puffed. Sprinkle with the confectioners' sugar.

Serves 4

Whole Wheat Huckleberry Pancakes

1 egg
1 cup buttermilk
2 tablespoons melted butter
3/4 cup whole wheat flour
1 tablespoon brown sugar
1 teaspoon baking powder
1/2 teaspoon baking soda
1/2 teaspoon salt
2 cups fresh huckleberries

Combine the egg, buttermilk, butter, whole wheat flour, brown sugar, baking powder, baking soda and salt in a bowl and mix well. Stir in the huckleberries. Pour onto a hot griddle. Turn when bubbles form along the edge. Cook until golden brown. Serve hot with fresh fruit.

Makes 8 (4-inch) pancakes

Sautéed Apples and Pork with Mustard Sauce

PORK STEAKS
1/2 cup flour
1/2 teaspoon pepper
1/4 teaspoon salt
4 (3-ounce) lean boneless pork steaks
2 tablespoons vegetable oil
2 tablespoons butter or margarine

APPLES
2 Jonagold or Golden Delicious apples, peeled, cored and sliced
2 tablespoons minced onion
1 tablespoon butter or margarine, melted

MUSTARD SAUCE
1 cup apple juice
1/2 cup dry white wine
1/2 cup plain low-fat yogurt
2 tablespoons Dijon mustard
1 tablespoon flour
1/4 teaspoon salt
1/4 teaspoon thyme

For the pork steaks, combine the flour, pepper and salt in a shallow dish. Coat the pork steaks with the flour mixture. Cook the prepared pork steaks in the hot oil and butter in a large skillet over medium heat until brown on both sides and the juices run clear. Remove to a heated serving platter.

For the apples, sauté the apples and onion in the melted butter in a skillet until tender. Spoon over the prepared pork steaks.

For the sauce, simmer the apple juice and wine in a skillet for 5 minutes, stirring occasionally. Combine the yogurt, Dijon mustard, flour, salt and thyme in a bowl and mix well. Add to the apple juice mixture. Simmer for 5 minutes, stirring until smooth. Spoon the sauce over the pork steaks and apples.

Serves 4

Apple-Stuffed Pork Chops

6 (1-inch-thick) pork loin chops
Seasoned salt to taste
Pepper to taste
Flour for coating
3 tart apples, peeled and sliced
1/4 cup packed brown sugar
1/4 teaspoon cloves
3 tablespoons lemon juice
2 tablespoons unsalted butter
1/2 cup dry white wine
1/3 cup raisins
1/4 cup slivered almonds
1/3 cup packed brown sugar
1/2 teaspoon cinnamon
1/4 teaspoon ginger

Sprinkle both sides of the pork chops with seasoned salt and pepper. Coat with flour. Cut a deep slit in the side of each pork chop to form a pocket. Combine the apples, 1/4 cup brown sugar, cloves and lemon juice in a bowl and mix well. Stuff the mixture into the pockets of the pork chops.

Brown the pork chops on both sides in the butter in a skillet. Stir in the wine, raisins, almonds, 1/3 cup brown sugar, cinnamon and ginger. Cook for 20 to 25 minutes or until the pork chops are cooked through, stirring occasionally.

Serves 6

Fresh Corn Chili

- 3/4 to 1 pound lean ground beef
- 1/2 to 1 cup chopped green bell pepper and red bell pepper (optional)
- 3 ears of fresh corn
- 1 (16-ounce) can kidney beans, drained
- 1 (15-ounce) can diced tomatoes with garlic and onion
- 2 cups salsa
- 1 cup shredded cheese
- 1/4 cup sliced green onions

Brown the ground beef and bell pepper in a large saucepan, stirring until the ground beef is crumbly; drain. Cut the corn kernels into a bowl using a sharp knife. Add the corn, kidney beans, tomatoes and salsa to the ground beef mixture and mix well. Simmer, uncovered, for 10 minutes, stirring occasionally. Ladle into soup bowls. Top with the cheese and green onions.

Note: You may substitute 1 (15-ounce) can whole kernel corn for the fresh corn if desired.

Serves 4 to 6

Eastern Washington Rack of Lamb

This recipe is from Chef Brad Masset at the Birchfield Manor in Yakima.

4 racks of lamb
Freshly ground pepper
 to taste
Kosher salt to taste
Vegetable oil
2 tablespoons soy sauce
2 tablespoons Dijon mustard
1 tablespoon vegetable oil
1 tablespoon apple juice
 concentrate
1 tablespoon brown sugar
1 teaspoon chopped garlic

Season the lamb with pepper and salt. Heat oil in a large skillet. Sauté the lamb until brown on all sides. Combine the soy sauce, Dijon mustard, 1 tablespoon oil, apple juice concentrate, brown sugar and garlic in a bowl and mix well. Baste the lamb with the sauce, coating liberally. Place the lamb on a rack in a large roasting pan. Roast at 400 degrees to the desired degree of doneness.

Serves 4

COOKING TEMPERATURES FOR LAMB

Rare 125° F
Medium-Rare 130° F
Medium 140° F
Ground Lamb 140° F

Chicken in Roasted Red Pepper Sauce

- 2 whole boneless chicken breasts, cut into 1/2-inch strips
- 1/2 cup flour
- 1/4 cup olive oil
- Salt to taste
- Pepper to taste
- 1/4 cup finely chopped onion
- 2 garlic cloves, minced
- 1 roasted red bell pepper, chopped
- 1 cup chopped peeled Roma tomatoes
- 1 cup quartered mushrooms
- 1/4 cup chicken broth
- 1/4 cup chardonnay
- 3/4 cup heavy cream
- 1/2 cup (or more) grated Parmesan cheese
- 16 ounces rigatoni or farfalle, cooked and drained

Coat the chicken with the flour. Sauté the chicken in the olive oil in a skillet until almost done. Sprinkle with salt and pepper. Remove to a plate. Sauté the onion and garlic in the skillet for 3 to 5 minutes. Add the roasted bell pepper, tomatoes and mushrooms. Sprinkle with salt and pepper. Stir in the chicken broth.

Add the cooked chicken. Stir in the chardonnay and cream. Bring to a light boil; reduce the heat to medium-low. Stir in the cheese. Cook until the sauce thickens, stirring frequently. Serve over the pasta and garnish with additional cheese.

Serves 6

Chicken Scaloppine with Zucchini

3 whole boneless chicken breasts
1/2 cup flour
1 1/2 teaspoons salt
1/4 teaspoon pepper
1/4 cup (1/2 stick) butter
1/2 cup walnut halves
3 zucchini, sliced
1/2 teaspoon oregano
1 teaspoon chopped fresh basil
2 cups light cream
1/4 cup grated Parmesan cheese
Chopped parsley to taste

Cut the chicken into 10 to 12 pieces. Pound the chicken between 2 sheets of plastic wrap until flat and thin. Combine the flour, salt and pepper. Reserve 2 tablespoons of the flour mixture. Coat the chicken in the remaining flour mixture, shaking off the excess. Heat the butter in a skillet until it sizzles. Sauté the chicken in the heated butter for 2 to 3 minutes per side or until cooked through. Remove the chicken with a slotted spoon and drain on paper towels. Keep warm. Sauté the walnuts in the skillet for 2 minutes. Remove to a bowl.

Sauté the zucchini in the skillet for 3 to 4 minutes or until tender-crisp. Toss with the walnuts. Arrange the mixture on a platter. Top with the chicken. Stir the reserved flour mixture, oregano and basil into the pan drippings in the skillet. Add the cream and cheese. Season with salt and pepper. Simmer for 5 minutes or until thick and bubbly, stirring frequently. Pour the sauce over the chicken. Sprinkle with parsley.

Serves 6

Rosemary Chicken Sandwiches with Lemon Caper Mayonnaise

LEMON CAPER MAYONNAISE
1/2 cup mayonnaise
1 tablespoon minced lemon zest
1 1/2 teaspoons chopped capers

ROSEMARY CHICKEN
4 to 6 chicken breasts
3/4 cup olive oil
3/4 cup balsamic vinegar
1/2 cup lemon juice
4 large garlic cloves, minced
1 tablespoon rosemary
1 teaspoon salt
1 teaspoon pepper
4 to 6 sourdough rolls
Roasted red peppers
Lettuce

FOR THE MAYONNAISE, combine the mayonnaise, lemon zest and capers in a bowl and mix well. Chill, covered, until ready to use.

FOR THE CHICKEN, place the chicken in a shallow glass dish. Combine the olive oil, vinegar, lemon juice, garlic, rosemary, salt and pepper in a food processor and pulse until blended. Pour the marinade over the chicken. Marinate, covered, in the refrigerator for 8 hours, turning occasionally. Broil or grill the chicken over hot coals for 8 to 10 minutes or until cooked through, turning once. Serve on sourdough rolls with the Lemon Caper Mayonnaise, roasted red peppers and lettuce.

Serves 4 to 6

Backyard Barbecued Chicken

1 (15-ounce) can tomato sauce
3 tablespoons chopped fresh parsley
1 garlic clove, minced
2 tablespoons sugar
2 teaspoons salt
1 teaspoon chili powder
1/4 teaspoon pepper
5 to 6 drops red pepper sauce
2 whole chickens, cut up

Combine the tomato sauce, parsley, garlic, sugar, salt, chili powder, pepper and red pepper sauce in a bowl and mix well. Grill the chicken bone side down over hot coals for 20 minutes. Turn the chicken. Brush with the barbecue sauce. Grill for 20 minutes. Turn the chicken. Brush with the barbecue sauce. Grill for 5 to 10 minutes longer or until cooked through.

Serves 6 to 8

Fresh Ginger-Marinated Salmon

3 to 4 pounds salmon fillets
1/3 cup dry white wine
3 tablespoons soy sauce
1 tablespoon dark sesame oil
2 teaspoons Dijon mustard
3 large garlic cloves
1 tablespoon grated fresh gingerroot
Seasoned salt to taste
Pepper to taste

Place the salmon in a shallow glass dish. Combine the wine, soy sauce, sesame oil, Dijon mustard, garlic, gingerroot, seasoned salt and pepper in a bowl and mix well. Pour the marinade over the salmon. Marinate, covered, in the refrigerator for 2 hours. Grill over hot coals until the fish flakes easily with a fork. You may substitute 1 teaspoon ground ginger for the gingerroot.

Serves 10

Northwest Maple Salmon

1/2 cup pure maple syrup
1 garlic clove, minced
1/4 teaspoon red pepper flakes
1 teaspoon chopped fresh gingerroot
Salmon fillet

Combine the maple syrup, garlic, red pepper flakes and gingerroot in a small saucepan. Bring to a boil, stirring occasionally. Place the salmon on a foil-lined baking sheet. Pour the maple syrup mixture over the salmon. Bake at 350 degrees until the fish flakes easily with a fork.

Serves 2

Broiled Salmon with Vanilla Beurre Blanc

4 shallots, minced
2 tablespoons white balsamic vinegar or rice vinegar
1/4 cup white wine
1 cup plus 1 tablespoon cold unsalted butter
2 vanilla beans
Salt to taste
Freshly ground pepper to taste
Dash of lemon juice
6 (4- to 5-ounce) salmon fillets

Combine the shallots, vinegar and white wine in a small nonreactive saucepan. Bring to a boil. Reduce the heat and simmer until the shallots are soft and the liquid is reduced to 1 tablespoon, stirring occasionally. Remove from the heat and pour through a fine mesh strainer. Return the strained liquid to the saucepan. Cook over low heat. Add the butter 1 tablespoon at a time, whisking continuously. Cut the vanilla bean into halves lengthwise and scrape the seeds into the saucepan. Sprinkle with salt and pepper. Stir in the lemon juice. Keep warm. Season the salmon with salt and pepper. Arrange skin side down on a foil-lined baking sheet. Broil for 6 to 8 minutes or until the salmon flakes easily with a fork.

Serves 6

Apple Bread with Streusel Topping

STREUSEL TOPPING
2 tablespoons flour
2 tablespoons sugar
1 teaspoon cinnamon
1 tablespoon butter

APPLE BREAD
2 cups flour
1 teaspoon baking soda
1/4 teaspoon salt
1/2 cup (1 stick) butter, softened
1 cup sugar
2 eggs
1 tablespoon lemon juice
2 teaspoons vanilla extract
2 Granny Smith apples, peeled and chopped

FOR THE TOPPING, combine the flour, sugar and cinnamon in a bowl. Cut in the butter until crumbly.

FOR THE BREAD, combine the flour, baking soda and salt in a bowl. Cream the butter and sugar in a mixing bowl. Beat in the eggs, lemon juice and vanilla. Add the flour mixture and stir just until moistened. Add the apples and stir gently to combine. Spoon 1/2 of the batter into a loaf pan. Sprinkle with 1/2 of the streusel topping. Spoon the remaining batter into the pan and sprinkle with the remaining topping. Bake at 350 degrees for 55 to 60 minutes or until a wooden pick inserted in the center comes out clean.

Makes 1 loaf

Chocolate Zucchini Bread

2 1/2 cups flour
1/2 cup baking cocoa
1 teaspoon baking powder
1 teaspoon baking soda
1 teaspoon salt
2 cups sugar
1 cup vegetable oil
3 eggs, beaten
2 tablespoons vanilla extract
2 cups finely shredded zucchini
1 cup (6 ounces) semisweet chocolate chips
1 cup chopped walnuts (optional)

Combine the flour, baking cocoa, baking powder, baking soda and salt in a bowl. Combine the sugar, oil, eggs and vanilla in a mixing bowl and beat until blended. Add the zucchini and mix well. Add the flour mixture and stir just until moistened. Stir in the chocolate chips and walnuts. Pour into 2 greased 5x9-inch loaf pans.

Bake at 350 degrees for 45 to 50 minutes or until a wooden pick inserted near the center comes out clean. Cool in the pan on a wire rack for 10 minutes. Remove the bread from the pans to a wire rack to cool completely.

Makes 2 loaves

Pumpkin Bread

- 3 1/2 cups flour
- 2 cups sugar
- 1 cup packed brown sugar
- 2 teaspoons baking soda
- 1 1/2 teaspoons salt
- 1 teaspoon cinnamon
- 1 teaspoon nutmeg
- 1 cup vegetable oil
- 4 eggs
- 2 cups canned pumpkin
- 2/3 cup water

Sift the flour, sugar, brown sugar, baking soda, salt, cinnamon and nutmeg into a large mixing bowl. Make a well in the center of the dry mixture. Add the oil, eggs, pumpkin and water and beat until blended. Pour into 2 large loaf pans. Bake at 350 degrees for 40 minutes. Cool in the pans for 10 minutes. Remove to a wire rack to cool completely.

Makes 2 loaves

Autumn Loaf Cake

CAKE
1/2 cup (1 stick) butter, softened
1 cup sugar
2 eggs
1 3/4 cups flour
1 teaspoon baking soda
1/2 teaspoon salt
1 teaspoon cinnamon
1/2 teaspoon nutmeg
1/4 teaspoon ginger
1/4 teaspoon ground cloves
3/4 cup pumpkin
3/4 cup chocolate chips

CINNAMON GLAZE
1/2 cup confectioners' sugar
1/8 teaspoon nutmeg
1/8 teaspoon cinnamon
1 to 2 tablespoons milk

FOR THE CAKE, cream the butter in a large mixing bowl. Add the sugar and beat until light and fluffy. Add the eggs 1 at a time, beating well after each addition. Combine the flour, baking soda, salt, cinnamon, nutmeg, ginger and cloves in a bowl and mix well. Add to the creamed mixture alternately with the pumpkin, beginning and ending with the dry ingredients and mixing well after each addition. Stir in the chocolate chips. Pour into a loaf pan. Bake at 350 degrees for 45 minutes or until a wooden pick inserted near the center comes out clean. Cool in the pan for 10 minutes. Remove to a wire rack to cool completely.

FOR THE GLAZE, combine the confectioners' sugar, nutmeg and cinnamon in a bowl. Add enough milk to make of a glaze consistency. Drizzle over the cooled cake.

Serves 8

Harvest Celebration Cake with Cream Cheese Frosting

CAKE

2 cups flour
2 cups sugar
1 1/2 teaspoons apple pie spice
1 teaspoon baking powder
1 teaspoon baking soda
1/4 teaspoon salt
2 cups coarsely shredded carrots
1 cup coarsely shredded apple
3/4 cup vegetable oil
4 eggs
1/2 cup chopped walnuts

CREAM CHEESE FROSTING

16 ounces cream cheese, softened
1 1/2 cups confectioners' sugar
2 tablespoons freshly squeezed orange juice
1/4 cup coarsely crushed apple chips

FOR THE CAKE, combine the flour, sugar, apple pie spice, baking powder, baking soda and salt in a large mixing bowl. Add the carrots, apple, oil and eggs and beat at low speed until combined. Beat at medium speed for 1 minute. Stir in the walnuts. Pour into 2 greased and lightly floured 9-inch cake pans. Bake at 350 degrees for 30 minutes or until a wooden pick inserted near the center comes out clean. Cool in the pans for 10 minutes. Remove to a wire rack to cool completely.

FOR THE FROSTING, beat the cream cheese, confectioners' sugar and orange juice in a mixing bowl until blended.

To assemble, place 1 cake layer on a serving plate. Spread the frosting over the top of the cake. Sprinkle with the apple chips. Top with the remaining cake layer. Spread the frosting over the top and side of the cake.

Note: You may decorate with whole apple chips and cinnamon sticks if desired. If apple pie spice is not available, substitute 1 teaspoon cinnamon and 1/2 teaspoon nutmeg.

Serves 12

Apple Cake with Hot Vanilla Sauce

APPLE CAKE
1 cup sugar
1/2 cup (1 stick) butter, softened
1 egg
1 cup flour
1 teaspoon baking soda
1/2 teaspoon cinnamon
1/2 teaspoon nutmeg
1/4 teaspoon salt
1 teaspoon vanilla extract
2 cups shredded apples
1/2 cup chopped pecans

HOT VANILLA SAUCE
1 cup sugar
1/2 cup evaporated milk
1/4 cup (1/2 stick) butter
1 1/2 teaspoons vanilla extract

For the cake, cream the sugar, butter, egg, flour, baking soda, cinnamon, nutmeg, salt and vanilla in a large mixing bowl. Stir in the apples and pecans. Pour into a greased 8- or 9-inch cake pan. Bake at 350 degrees for 40 minutes.

For the sauce, combine the sugar, evaporated milk, butter and vanilla in a saucepan. Cook for 5 minutes over direct heat or for 20 minutes in a double boiler, stirring frequently. Pour over the warm cake.

Serves 12

Knobby Apple Cake

1 cup sugar
1/4 cup shortening or butter
1 egg
1 teaspoon vanilla extract
1 cup flour
1/2 teaspoon baking powder
1/2 teaspoon baking soda
1/2 teaspoon salt
1/2 teaspoon cinnamon
1/2 teaspoon nutmeg
2 1/2 cups chopped or shredded peeled apples
1/4 cup chopped walnuts (optional)

Cream the sugar, shortening and egg in a large mixing bowl. Add the vanilla and beat until blended. Add the flour, baking powder, baking soda, salt, cinnamon and nutmeg and mix well. Stir in the apples and walnuts. Spoon into a greased 8-inch cake pan. Bake at 350 degrees for 45 minutes. Serve hot or cold with vanilla ice cream.

Note: You may add 1/4 cup coconut and 1/4 cup finely chopped raisins for a heartier cake.

Serves 12

Carrot Walnut Cake

2 cups flour
2 teaspoons baking soda
1/8 teaspoon salt
2 teaspoons cinnamon
2 teaspoons nutmeg
4 eggs
1 1/4 cups sugar
1 1/2 cups vegetable oil
2 teaspoons vanilla extract
3 cups shredded carrots
2/3 cup walnut halves, chopped

Sift together the flour, baking soda, salt, cinnamon and nutmeg. Beat the eggs in a mixing bowl until thickened. Add the sugar gradually, beating until thickened. Add the oil gradually, beating constantly. Stir in the vanilla. Add the flour mixture, carrots and walnuts and mix well. Pour into a greased and floured 9×13-inch cake pan. Bake at 325 degrees for 45 to 60 minutes or until a wooden pick inserted near the center comes out clean.

Remove to a wire rack and cool completely. You may frost with Cream Cheese Frosting if desired (pages 109 and 151).

Serves 10

Apple Tart

TART
6 tablespoons unsalted butter
1 cup flour
2 tablespoons sugar
3 tablespoons cold water

FILLING
4 Golden Delicious apples, peeled
1/4 cup sugar
3 tablespoons butter, chopped
1 tablespoon Calvados brandy or apricot brandy

GLAZE
3 tablespoons apricot jam
1 tablespoon water

For the tart, combine the butter, flour and sugar in a food processor and process until mixture resembles coarse meal. Add the water gradually, processing constantly until the mixture forms a soft dough. Chill, wrapped in plastic wrap, for 1 hour. Roll the dough into a 10 1/2-inch circle on a lightly floured surface. Fit into a 9-inch tart pan, trimming and fluting the edge. Chill, covered, in the freezer while preparing the filling.

For the filling, cut the apples into halves lengthwise. Place the apples cut side down on a cutting board. Cut into slices, maintaining the shape of the apples. Fan the apple slices in the tart shell. Sprinkle with the sugar. Dot with the butter. Sprinkle with the brandy. Bake at 375 degrees for 45 minutes or until golden brown.

For the glaze, combine the jam and water in a saucepan. Cook until blended, stirring constantly. Pour over the warm tart. Bake at 375 degrees for 5 minutes. Let stand until cool.

Serves 6 to 8

French Apple Pie

APPLE FILLING
2/3 cup orange juice
1 tablespoon butter
1/2 cup sugar
1/2 teaspoon grated orange zest
1/2 teaspoon cinnamon
1/4 teaspoon nutmeg
4 apples, peeled and sliced
4 1/2 teaspoons cornstarch
4 1/2 teaspoons water
2 tablespoons lemon juice
1 baked (9-inch) pie shell

CHEESE FILLING
8 ounces cream cheese, softened
1/2 cup sugar
1/2 teaspoon grated orange zest
1 egg
1/2 cup chopped almonds
1/2 cup shredded coconut

For the apple filling, combine the orange juice, butter, sugar, orange zest, cinnamon and nutmeg in a saucepan and bring to a boil. Boil until the sugar dissolves, stirring constantly. Add the apples. Boil gently for 10 minutes or just until the apples are tender, stirring occasionally.

Combine the cornstarch and water in a small bowl and mix well. Add to the apple mixture. Boil until the mixture thickens, stirring constantly. Stir in the lemon juice. Remove from the heat and let stand until cool. Pour into the pie shell.

For the cheese filling, beat the cream cheese, sugar and orange zest in a mixing bowl until light and fluffy. Beat in the egg. Spoon over the apple filling. Sprinkle with the almonds and coconut. Bake at 350 degrees for 20 to 25 minutes or until light brown on top. Chill, covered, before serving.

Serves 8

Apple Crisp

8 cups chopped apples
1/2 cup sugar
1 teaspoon cinnamon
1 cup quick-cooking oats
1 cup packed brown sugar
1 cup flour
1 teaspoon cinnamon
2/3 cup margarine

Combine the apples, sugar and 1 teaspoon cinnamon in a bowl and toss to mix. Arrange the apple mixture in a greased 9×13-inch baking pan. Combine the oats, brown sugar, flour and 1 teaspoon cinnamon in a bowl and mix well. Cut in the margarine until crumbly. Sprinkle over the apple mixture. Bake at 375 degrees for 35 minutes or until the apples are tender and the topping is golden brown. Serve with vanilla ice cream or wedges of sharp Cheddar cheese.

Serves 10

Cheesy Golden Apple Crumble

4 large Golden Delicious apples, peeled and sliced
1/2 cup sugar
1 teaspoon cinnamon
2 tablespoons water
1 cup flour
1/2 cup sugar
1/2 teaspoon salt
1/2 cup (2 ounces) shredded Cheddar cheese
1/2 cup (1 stick) melted butter

Combine the apples, 1/2 cup sugar, cinnamon and water in a bowl and toss to mix. Arrange the apple mixture in a buttered 9×9-inch baking pan. Combine the flour, 1/2 cup sugar, salt, cheese and butter in a bowl and mix until crumbly. Sprinkle over the apple mixture. Bake at 350 degrees for 45 minutes.

Serves 4 to 6

Caramel Apple Sundae Cheesecake

CRUST
1/3 cup butter
1/3 cup sugar
1 egg
1 1/4 cups flour

FILLING
16 ounces cream cheese, softened
1/3 cup sugar
2 tablespoons flour
3 eggs
1/2 cup sour cream
1 cup chopped peeled apples
1/3 cup sugar
3/4 teaspoon cinnamon
1/2 cup caramel ice cream topping
1/4 cup chopped pecans

For the crust, cream the butter and sugar in a mixing bowl until light and fluffy. Add the egg and beat until blended. Add the flour and mix well. Spread over the bottom of a 9-inch springform pan. Bake at 450 degrees for 10 minutes.

For the filling, combine the cream cheese, 1/3 cup sugar and flour in a food processor and process until smooth. Add the eggs 1 at a time, processing until smooth after each addition. Add the sour cream and process until smooth. Toss the apples, 1/3 cup sugar and cinnamon in a bowl. Add the sour cream mixture to the apples and stir gently to combine. Spoon over the prepared crust. Swirl in the caramel topping. Bake at 350 degrees for 1 hour. Chill, covered, in the refrigerator. Top with additional caramel topping if desired. Sprinkle with the pecans.

Serves 12

Spray your measuring cup with nonstick cooking spray before measuring syrup, molasses, peanut butter, or honey. You will get a more accurate measurement, and the cup will wash much easier.

Pumpkin Bread Pudding

PUDDING
1 (1-pound) loaf unsliced white bread
1 pint half-and-half
6 eggs
1 cup cooked pumpkin or winter squash
1 tablespoon vanilla extract
2/3 cup sugar
2 teaspoons cinnamon
2 teaspoons ginger
1/2 teaspoon cloves
1/2 teaspoon salt
1 cup raisins

GINGER SAUCE
1 cup half-and-half
1 teaspoon chopped fresh gingerroot
3 eggs
2 tablespoons sugar

FOR THE PUDDING, trim the crust from the bread and cut the bread into 1/2-inch cubes. Whisk the half-and-half and eggs in a large bowl. Add the pumpkin, vanilla, sugar, cinnamon, ginger, cloves and salt and whisk until blended. Stir in the bread cubes and raisins. Let stand for 5 minutes or until most of the liquid is absorbed. Spoon into a buttered 9x9-inch baking pan. Bake at 350 degrees for 35 to 40 minutes or until firm to the touch.

FOR THE SAUCE, combine the half-and-half and gingerroot in a saucepan and mix well. Bring to a boil, stirring occasionally. Whisk the eggs and sugar in a bowl. Add the half-and-half mixture slowly, whisking constantly until blended. Pour the mixture into the saucepan. Cook over low heat until the mixture thickens slightly and coats the back of a spoon, stirring constantly. Chill, covered, until thickened. Strain out the gingerroot before serving.

TO SERVE, spoon the sauce over the bread pudding.

Serves 8

Pumpkin Cheesecake Bars

PECAN CRUST
1 cup flour
1/3 cup packed brown sugar
5 tablespoons butter
1/2 cup finely chopped pecans

BARS
8 ounces cream cheese, softened
1/2 cup canned pumpkin
2 eggs, lightly beaten
3/4 cup sugar
1 1/2 teaspoons cinnamon
1 teaspoon allspice
1 teaspoon vanilla extract
32 pecan halves (optional)

For the crust, combine the flour and brown sugar in a bowl and mix well. Cut in the butter until crumbly. Stir in the pecans. Reserve 3/4 cup of the mixture for the topping. Press the remaining mixture over the bottom of an 8×8-inch baking pan. Bake at 350 degrees for 15 minutes. Let stand until slightly cooled.

For the bars, combine the cream cheese, pumpkin, eggs, sugar, cinnamon, allspice and vanilla in a mixing bowl and beat until smooth. Pour over the prepared crust. Sprinkle with the reserved crumb mixture. Bake at 350 degrees for 35 to 40 minutes or until slightly firm. Cool on a wire rack. Cut into squares and cut each square into triangles. Garnish each triangle with a pecan half.

Makes 5 to 6 dozen bars

Caramel Apple Cookies

COOKIES
- 1 1/4 cups packed brown sugar
- 1/2 cup shortening
- 1 egg
- 1/2 cup apple juice
- 2 1/4 cups whole wheat flour or all-purpose flour
- 1 teaspoon baking soda
- 2 teaspoons cinnamon
- 1 teaspoon cloves
- 1/4 teaspoon salt
- 1 large tart apple, peeled and shredded
- 3/4 cup raisins

CARAMEL FROSTING
- 1/3 cup packed brown sugar
- 2 tablespoons margarine
- 2 tablespoons water
- 1 3/4 cups sifted confectioners' sugar
- 1/4 cup chopped walnuts (optional)

For the cookies, combine the brown sugar and shortening in a mixing bowl and beat until blended. Add the egg and beat for 1 minute. Add the apple juice and beat at low speed until blended. Combine the flour, baking soda, cinnamon, cloves and salt in a bowl and mix well. Add to the shortening mixture and beat at low speed until blended. Stir in the apples and raisins. Drop by rounded teaspoonfuls 1 1/2 inches apart onto an ungreased cookie sheet. Bake at 350 degrees for 8 minutes or until the edges are light brown. Cool on wire racks.

For the frosting, heat the brown sugar, margarine and water in a saucepan over medium heat until the sugar dissolves, stirring constantly. Remove from the heat and stir in the confectioners' sugar. Frost the cooled cookies immediately. Stir in a small amount of milk if frosting begins to harden before using. Sprinkle with the walnuts.

Makes 6 dozen cookies

Winter Harvest

Pears to Wine

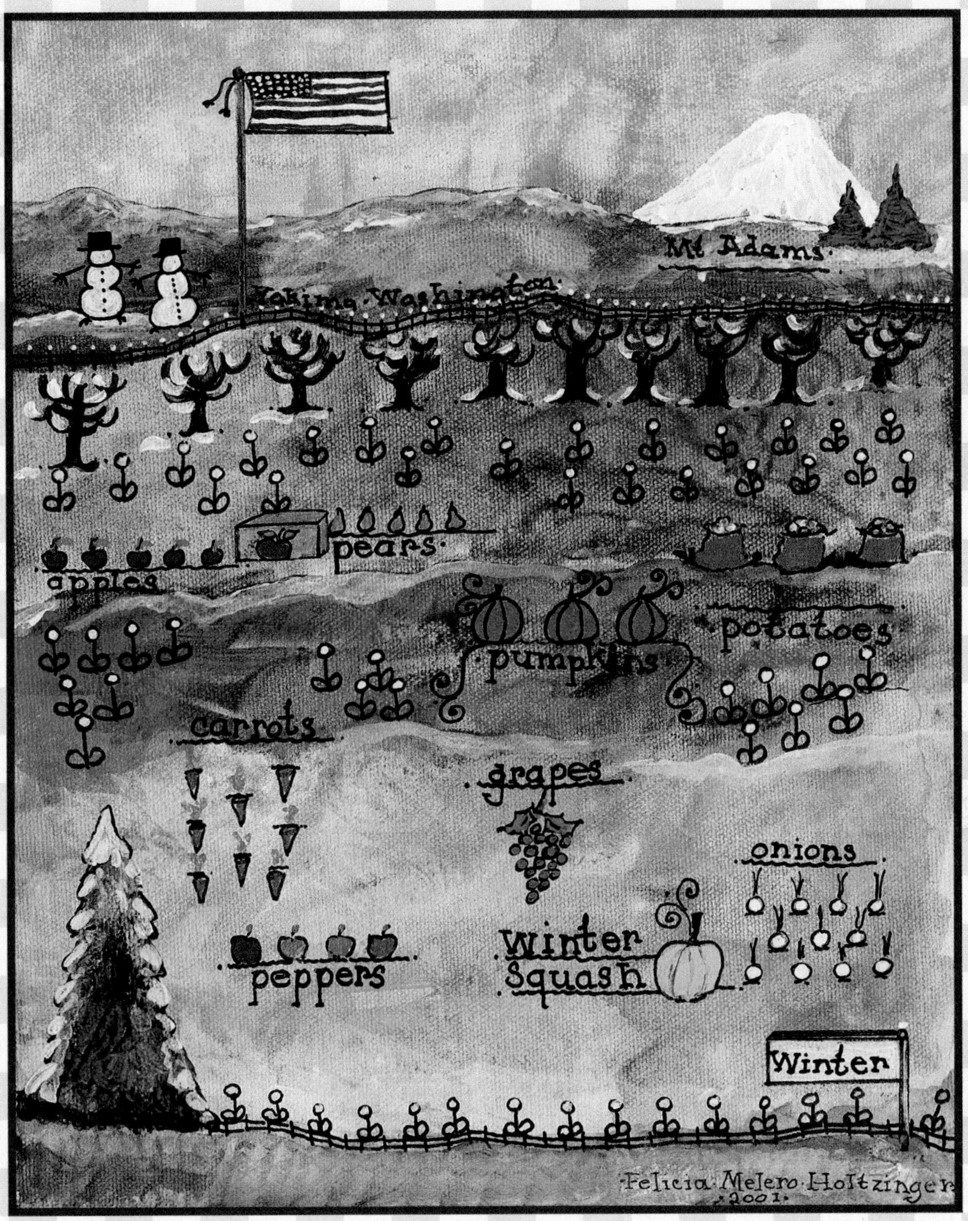

Mt Adams
Yakima Washington
pears
apples
pumpkins
potatoes
carrots
grapes
onions
Winter
Squash
peppers
Winter
Felicia Melero Holtzinger
2001

Winter Harvest

As the holiday season begins, the final harvest
of the Yakima Valley comes to an end.
The warm days give way to cool.
Savory soups and stews simmer on the stove
and gentle, warm fires blaze in the fireplace.
Pears, wine grapes, hearty potatoes, and
winter squash round out our growing season.
As the days close, we raise a toast to health,
family, friends, and good food.

Dried Cranberry and Mango Chutney

$1/2$ cup dried cranberries
$1/4$ cup water
2 tablespoons sugar
1 tablespoon finely chopped fresh gingerroot
$3/4$ cup chopped mango

Combine the cranberries, water, sugar and gingerroot in a saucepan. Bring to a boil, stirring occasionally. Remove from the heat and let stand, covered, for 15 minutes. Add the mango and mix well. Spoon into a bowl. Chill, covered, for 2 hours or more before serving. Serve with soft cheese or cream cheese, sliced apples, crackers or toasted baguette slices.

Makes 1 $1/2$ cups

Mango ripeness can be determined by smelling or squeezing the mango. A ripe mango will have a full, fruity aroma around the stem end. They are ready to eat when slightly soft to the touch and yielding to gentle pressure. The mango will have a yellowish tinge to it when ripe, but there can be a color combination of red, green, yellow, or orange. A mango can ripen at room temperature on a kitchen counter. To accelerate the ripening process, place in a paper bag overnight. Once ripened, the mango should be eaten or refrigerated.

Artichoke and Parmesan Strudel

2 (10-ounce) cans artichokes, drained and chopped
1 1/2 cups cottage cheese
1 1/2 cups freshly grated Parmesan cheese
3 eggs
1/2 cup finely chopped green onions
1/2 cup fresh bread crumbs
3/4 teaspoon tarragon
Freshly ground pepper to taste
16 ounces phyllo dough
1 cup (2 sticks) melted butter

Combine the artichokes, cottage cheese, Parmesan cheese, eggs, green onions, bread crumbs, tarragon and pepper in a bowl and mix well. Roll out the phyllo dough onto a large sheet of foil. Cut the dough into a 12×16-inch rectangle. Brush 1 phyllo sheet with melted butter. Top with another phyllo sheet and brush with melted butter. Repeat the process 6 times, working quickly. Keep the remaining portion of unused dough covered with a damp towel to prevent it from drying out while working.

Mound 2 (scant) cups of the artichoke mixture crosswise 3 inches from the short end of the rectangle, folding over to enclose the filling. Roll as for a jelly roll, brushing with melted butter and sealing the edge. Repeat the process with the remaining phyllo dough and artichoke mixture 2 times. Arrange the rolls seam side down 6 inches apart on a baking sheet. Brush the rolls with melted butter. Bake at 400 degrees for 25 to 30 minutes or until golden brown. Let cool for 5 minutes before slicing.

Serves 12

Two-Olive Crostini

This will make an impressive addition to your favorite appetizer sampler.

2 garlic cloves
1/2 cup grated Parmesan cheese
1/4 cup (1/2 stick) butter, softened
2 tablespoons olive oil
1/2 cup pitted kalamata olives or gaeta olives, coarsely chopped
1/2 cup green olives with pimento, coarsely chopped
1/2 cup (2 ounces) shredded Monterey Jack cheese
1/4 cup chopped fresh parsley
1 baguette

Mince the garlic in a food processor. Add the Parmesan cheese, butter and olive oil and process until mixture is of a paste consistency. Combine the garlic mixture with the olives in a bowl and mix well. Add the Monterey Jack cheese and parsley and mix well. Cut the baguette into thin slices. Spread each slice with the olive mixture. Arrange the prepared baguette slices on a baking sheet. Bake at 350 degrees until the cheese melts. Serve immediately.

Note: You may prepare the olive mixture 1 day in advance and chill, covered, until ready to serve.

Serves 12

Apple Ratatouille on Crostini

- 1/2 cup walnut oil
- 1/4 cup vegetable oil
- 2 1/2 cups finely chopped celery
- 2 cups finely chopped red onions
- 4 cups chopped peeled apples, such as Washington Granny Smith, Golden Delicious, Braeburn or Fuji
- 4 cups chopped zucchini
- 2 cups chopped yellow squash
- 2 tablespoons minced garlic
- 1 1/2 cups canned diced tomatoes, drained
- 3/4 cup coarsely chopped walnuts
- 1 tablespoon salt
- 1 1/2 teaspoon pepper
- 1 teaspoon nutmeg
- 1 teaspoon turmeric
- 1/4 cup chopped fresh basil
- 48 baguette slices, grilled or toasted

Combine the walnut oil and vegetable oil in a bowl. Heat 1/4 cup of the oil mixture in a heavy skillet. Sauté the celery and onions in the hot oil over medium heat until tender and brown. Remove the celery mixture to a bowl. Heat 1/4 cup of the oil mixture in the skillet. Sauté the apples in the hot oil until tender and golden. Add the cooked apples to the celery mixture. Heat the remaining 1/4 cup oil mixture in the skillet. Sauté the zucchini, yellow squash and garlic in the hot oil until tender. Add the apple mixture and toss to combine. Stir in the tomatoes, walnuts, salt, pepper, nutmeg and turmeric. Cook over medium heat for 5 to 10 minutes or until the mixture is thickened, stirring frequently. Stir in the basil. Cook for 1 to 2 minutes. Spoon 2 tablespoons of the ratatouille onto each baguette slice and serve immediately.

Serves 24

Parmesan Toast

1 cup mayonnaise
1/2 cup chopped onion
1/2 cup grated Parmesan cheese
1/2 teaspoon paprika
1/2 teaspoon Worcestershire sauce
1 loaf French bread

Combine the mayonnaise, onion, cheese, paprika and Worcestershire sauce in a bowl and mix well. Slice the bread into halves lengthwise. Spread each half with the onion mixture. Arrange on a baking sheet. Broil for 5 minutes. Cut into slices and serve immediately.

Makes 8 servings

Marinated Mushrooms

1 1/2 cups olive oil
2/3 cup wine vinegar
2 garlic cloves
12 peppercorns
2 bay leaves
3 teaspoons salt
1 teaspoon basil
1 1/2 teaspoons sugar
3 pounds assorted mushrooms

Combine the olive oil, vinegar, garlic, peppercorns, bay leaves, salt, basil and sugar in a saucepan. Bring to a boil, stirring frequently. Reduce the heat and simmer, covered, for 10 minutes. Add the mushrooms and stir until coated. Cook over medium heat for 3 to 5 minutes or until tender, stirring occasionally. Spoon into a shallow dish. Chill, covered, until ready to serve. Drain the marinade and remove the bay leaves before serving.

Serves 16

Apple and Pear Salad with Orange Vinaigrette

SALAD
6 to 8 cups mixed salad greens, rinsed, drained and chilled
2 cups julienned apples
2 cups julienned pears
1 cup (4 ounces) crumbled Gorgonzola cheese
1 cup pecan halves, lightly roasted

ORANGE VINAIGRETTE
1/2 cup olive oil
1/2 cup walnut oil
1/2 cup tarragon vinegar
1 tablespoon frozen orange juice concentrate
Salt to taste
Freshly ground pepper to taste

FOR THE SALAD, arrange the greens on salad plates. Arrange the apples and pears over the greens. Sprinkle with the cheese and pecans.

FOR THE VINAIGRETTE, combine the olive oil, walnut oil, vinegar, orange juice concentrate, salt and pepper in a bowl and whisk to blend. Pour over the salad and toss to coat well.

Serves 6 to 8

Nut oils are made primarily in France. Walnut oil has the most delicate aroma and taste. To keep nut oils fresh, store them, tightly covered, in a cool place but not in the refrigerator. Though light does not seem to affect the flavor, heat does. Stored carefully, the oils will remain fresh tasting for many months.

Pear and Bleu Cheese Salad with Caramelized Almonds

DRESSING
1/2 cup vegetable oil
3 tablespoons vinegar
1/4 cup sugar
1/2 teaspoon celery seeds

CARAMELIZED ALMONDS
1/4 cup almonds, whole or sliced
2 tablespoons sugar

SALAD
4 cups torn leaf lettuce
1 pear, chopped or sliced
2 ounces bleu cheese, crumbled

For the dressing, combine the oil, vinegar, sugar and celery seeds in a jar with a tight-fitting lid. Shake until blended. Chill in the refrigerator for 45 minutes.

For the caramelized almonds, combine the almonds and sugar in a nonstick skillet. Cook over medium heat until the sugar melts and the almonds are coated, stirring constantly. Remove from the heat and let stand until cool. Break up the almonds and store in a covered container at room temperature until ready to serve.

For the salad, combine the lettuce, pear, bleu cheese and caramelized almonds in a large bowl. Add the dressing and toss to coat well.

Serves 4

Fresh Winter Pear Salad with Whole Wheat Croutons

With the mild, sweet flavor and smooth texture of pears, an otherwise ordinary salad instantly becomes special.

RED WINE VINEGAR DRESSING
3 tablespoons vegetable oil
1 tablespoon red wine vinegar
1 tablespoon lemon juice
1/4 teaspoon salt
1/8 teaspoon pepper
Dash of Worcestershire sauce

WHOLE WHEAT CROUTONS
1 tablespoon melted butter or margarine
1/2 cup whole wheat bread cubes
Garlic powder to taste

PEAR SALAD
2 cups mixed salad greens
1/2 cup sliced mushrooms
1/2 cup sliced radishes
1/3 cup bean sprouts
1 Northwest Bosc pear or Anjou pear, sliced

FOR THE DRESSING, combine the oil, vinegar, lemon juice, salt, pepper and Worcestershire sauce in a bowl and whisk to blend.

FOR THE CROUTONS, combine the butter and bread cubes in an 8×8-inch baking pan and stir to coat. Sprinkle with garlic powder. Bake at 250 degrees for 20 to 30 minutes or until the bread cubes are toasted.

FOR THE SALAD, combine the salad greens, mushrooms, radishes and bean sprouts in a salad bowl and toss to mix. Add the pear slices, dressing and croutons and toss gently to coat. Serve immediately.

Serves 4

Pear and Salmon Salad with Lemon Dressing

Northwest pears pair fabulously with another favorite of the Northwest—salmon. This appetizing salad is a good choice for a light meal.

LEMON DRESSING
3 tablespoons olive oil
3 tablespoons lemon juice
1/2 teaspoon salt
1/8 teaspoon pepper

SALAD
Romaine or red leaf lettuce
8 ounces smoked salmon
2 Northwest pears, sliced into eighths
2 tomatoes, sliced
1 cucumber, chopped
1 cup sliced mushrooms
Lemon wedges

For the dressing, combine the olive oil, lemon juice, salt and pepper in a bowl and whisk to blend.

For the salad, line 4 dinner plates with the lettuce. Arrange the salmon, pears, tomatoes, cucumber and mushrooms on the lettuce-lined plates. Garnish with the lemon wedges. Serve with Lemon Dressing on the side.

Serves 4

Pear and Shrimp Salad with Honey Yogurt Dressing

HONEY YOGURT DRESSING
2 tablespoons honey
2 teaspoons vinegar
1 teaspoon celery seeds
1/4 teaspoon salt
1 cup (8 ounces) plain yogurt

SALAD
1 (8-ounce) can pineapple chunks
1 or 2 ripe Anjou pears
Lettuce
1 1/2 cups cooked tiny shrimp
1 cucumber, scored and sliced
Sliced radishes
Alfalfa sprouts

FOR THE DRESSING, combine the honey, vinegar, celery seeds, salt and yogurt in a bowl and mix well. Chill, covered, until ready to serve.

FOR THE SALAD, drain the pineapple, reserving the syrup. Core and slice the pears. Brush the pear slices with the reserved syrup to prevent browning. Line a serving plate with the lettuce. Arrange the pears, pineapple, shrimp, cucumber and radishes on the lettuce-lined plate. Garnish with alfalfa sprouts. Serve with Honey Yogurt dressing on the side.

Serves 4 to 6

Bleu Cheese Potato Salad

The bleu cheese adds a great and unique flavor to this potato salad.

4 pounds red potatoes
1/4 cup cider vinegar
2 tablespoons Dijon mustard
Salt to taste
Pepper to taste
2/3 cup olive oil
1/4 cup chopped shallots
2 tablespoons chopped fresh parsley
1/2 cup crumbled bleu cheese
1/2 cup half-and-half
5 slices bacon, crisp-cooked and crumbled
3 tablespoons chives

Combine the potatoes with enough water to cover in a saucepan. Bring to a boil; boil just until tender. Drain and cool the potatoes. Slice the potatoes and arrange on a serving platter. Combine the vinegar, Dijon mustard, salt and pepper in a food processor and process until blended. Add the olive oil in a fine stream, processing constantly until smooth. Add the shallots and parsley and process until mixed well. Pour 1/2 cup of the dressing over the sliced potatoes. Add the bleu cheese and half-and-half to the remaining dressing and mix well. Spoon over the potatoes. Garnish with the bacon and chives. Serve warm or at room temperature.

Note: To whiten the potatoes, you may add a few drops of lemon juice to the water when boiling.

Serves 8

Apple Fennel Soup

When the impulse strikes, here is a flavorful puréed soup that can be prepared in just 30 minutes.

1 (14-ounce) can reduced-sodium chicken broth
2 cups water
1/2 cup white wine
2 Golden Delicious apples, peeled and chopped
1 cup thinly sliced carrots
1 small onion, thinly sliced
1/2 cup chopped fresh fennel
1 bay leaf
1/4 teaspoon thyme
6 peppercorns
Plain low-fat yogurt (optional)

Combine the chicken broth, water, wine, apples, carrots, onion, fennel, bay leaf, thyme and peppercorns in a large saucepan. Bring to a boil, stirring occasionally. Reduce the heat and simmer, covered, for 20 minutes. Strain the soup, reserving the liquid. Remove the bay leaf from the vegetable mixture. Purée the vegetable mixture in a blender. Add the reserved liquid and process until smooth. Reheat the soup if needed. Ladle into soup bowls and top with a dollop of yogurt.

Serves 4

Fennel is a member of the parsley family. It is often referred to as sweet anise; however, fennel is more aromatic and sweeter than anise. Used when making Italian sausage, fennel also goes well with fish and in curry mixes. Accentuate the flavor of fennel seeds by toasting them.

Mexican Soup

4 slices bacon, chopped
3/4 cup chopped onion
3/4 cup chopped celery
1 garlic clove, minced
1 (16-ounce) can refried beans
1 (4-ounce) can diced green chiles
1 (13-ounce) can chicken broth
2 dashes of Tabasco sauce
1/4 teaspoon pepper
1 cup (4 ounces) shredded sharp Cheddar cheese

Cook the bacon in a large deep skillet until crisp. Add the onion and celery to the skillet and sauté until tender. Add the garlic and sauté until tender. Add the beans, green chiles, chicken broth, Tabasco sauce and pepper. Stir to mix well. Bring to a simmer and cook until heated through. Ladle into warm bowls and top with the cheese. Serve with colorful tortilla chips and guacamole on the side.

Serves 4

Mexican-Style Hot Chocolate

1 (3-ounce) wheel Mexican-style sweet chocolate, chopped
1/2 gallon milk
1 vanilla bean (optional)
1 cup Kahlúa or other coffee liqueur (optional)
Whipped cream for topping

Heat the chocolate and milk in a saucepan over medium-high heat, stirring frequently until the chocolate is melted. Split the vanilla bean open and scrape the seeds into the milk mixture. Cook until the mixture is very hot. Add the liqueur and whisk to mix well. Pour into mugs and top with the whipped cream. Serve immediately.

Note: Mexican-style sweet chocolate can be found in Latin food markets. It is high in sugar and flavored with cinnamon and sometimes almonds. Ibarra and Abuelita are two popular brands.

Serves 8

Carrots in Maple Dill Sauce

1/2 cup (1 stick) butter
1/2 cup maple syrup
3 pounds carrots, cut into bite-size pieces
1 tablespoon chopped fresh dill weed

Melt the butter with the syrup in a saucepan over medium heat. Cook for about 5 minutes or until the mixture begins to boil. Steam the carrots over boiling water for about 7 minutes or until tender-crisp; drain. Spoon the carrots into a serving bowl and pour the butter mixture over the top. Sprinkle with the dill weed and toss to coat well. Serve immediately.

Serves 6

Oven-Roasted Winter Vegetables

1 large sweet potato, peeled and cut into 1-inch cubes
1 fennel bulb, trimmed and cut into wedges
8 ounces new potatoes, quartered
6 ounces shiitake mushrooms, trimmed and cut into halves
4 large shallots, peeled and quartered
2 tablespoons walnut oil
2 tablespoons balsamic vinegar
1 teaspoon coarse salt

Combine the sweet potato, fennel, new potatoes, mushrooms and shallots with the walnut oil, 1 tablespoon of the balsamic vinegar and salt in a large roasting pan. Toss to coat well. Roast at 425 degrees for 30 to 35 minutes or until the vegetables are lightly browned and tender, stirring twice. Spoon the vegetables into a large serving bowl and toss with the remaining 1 tablespoon balsamic vinegar. Serve warm.

Note: High quality walnut oil will offer the richest flavor. You can find it in gourmet food stores.

Serves 4 to 6

Acorn Squash with Cranberries

2 medium acorn squash
2 tablespoons butter or margarine
1/4 teaspoon ground cloves
1 cup cranberries
1/2 cup cranberry juice cocktail or apricot nectar
1 teaspoon orange zest
1/3 cup maple syrup
1/4 cup chopped walnuts or hazelnuts, toasted (optional)

Slice the squash crosswise into 1/2-inch-thick slices; remove the seeds. Heat the butter in a skillet over medium-high heat. Add the squash and cloves to the butter. Cook, covered, for 8 minutes or until the squash begins to soften, stirring occasionally. Add the cranberries, cranberry juice cocktail and orange zest. Bring to a boil. Reduce the heat and simmer, covered, for 5 to 10 minutes or until the squash is tender. Remove from the heat. Stir in the maple syrup and walnuts. Serve immediately.

Serves 6 to 8

Acorn squash is an edible gourd that grows on a vine. It has a sweet, nutty flavor. A ripe acorn squash should weigh between 1 to 3 pounds and have no soft spots. Look for a good color balance of green and orange when choosing an acorn squash. Too much orange will indicate a dry, stringy squash.

Swiss Onion Gratin

4 cups sliced onions
2 tablespoons butter
1/2 (10-ounce) can cream of chicken soup
1/2 cup milk
1 teaspoon Worcestershire sauce
1/4 cup shredded Swiss cheese
4 slices French bread
1 teaspoon parsley
1 tablespoon sesame seeds

Sauté the onions in the butter in a skillet until tender. Spoon into a shallow baking dish. Combine the soup, milk and Worcestershire sauce in a small bowl and mix well. Pour over the onions. Top with the Swiss cheese.

Cut the bread slices into triangles and butter the tops. Arrange over the cheese layer. Sprinkle with the parsley and sesame seeds. Bake at 350 degrees for 25 minutes or until bubbly.

Serves 6 to 8

Baked Sweet Onions

2 medium Walla Walla sweet onions, sliced 1/2 inch thick
1 cup mayonnaise
1/2 cup grated Parmesan cheese
1 1/2 teaspoons seasoned salt

Arrange the onion slices 1 inch apart in a baking dish. Combine the remaining ingredients in a small bowl and mix well. Spread 1 heaping tablespoon of the mixture on top of each onion slice. Bake, covered, at 350 degrees for 35 to 40 minutes or until tender. Bake, uncovered, for 5 minutes or until browned.

Serves 6

Buffet Potatoes

4 medium potatoes
3 tablespoons butter, sliced
1 teaspoon salt
1/2 teaspoon pepper
1/2 teaspoon parsley
1/2 cup (2 ounces) shredded sharp Cheddar cheese
1 tablespoon finely chopped onion
1/2 cup cream

Slice the potatoes into thin 1/4-inch strips. Layer down the center of a foil-lined shallow baking dish. Top the potatoes with butter. Sprinkle with the salt, pepper, parsley, cheese and onion. Pour the cream over the top. Seal the edges of the foil tightly. Bake at 400 degrees for 90 minutes. Serve hot.

Serves 4 to 8

Savory Herb-Roasted Pears

These elegant roasted pears will highlight any affair. Serve with chicken, turkey, pork, or add to a fresh salad. Northwest Anjou pears, balsamic vinegar, olive oil, and herbs make a delicious combination that is a treat to the palate. Also wonderful served warm with a soft cheese course for dessert.

- 2 tablespoons balsamic vinegar
- 2 tablespoons olive oil
- 1 teaspoon Dijon mustard
- 1 teaspoon minced fresh thyme
- 1/2 teaspoon minced fresh rosemary
- 1/4 teaspoon salt
- 1/4 teaspoon freshly ground pepper
- 1/8 teaspoon ground sage
- 4 firm ripe Northwest Anjou Pears, peeled and quartered

Combine the balsamic vinegar, olive oil, Dijon mustard, thyme, rosemary, salt, pepper and sage in a small bowl and mix well. Brush the pears with the mixture. Arrange the pears on a greased rack in a broiler pan. Bake at 425 degrees for 12 to 15 minutes or until tender, brushing once after 6 minutes. Serve warm.

Serves 8

Apple Valley Stew

3 tablespoons flour
1/2 teaspoon cumin
1/2 teaspoon chili powder
1/2 teaspoon garlic powder
1/4 teaspoon cinnamon
1 1/2 to 2 pounds lean beef chuck, cut into cubes
2 tablespoons vegetable oil
1 cup beef broth
1/2 cup apple juice
6 small white potatoes, peeled and quartered
2 sweet potatoes, peeled and cubed
1 green bell pepper, cut into strips
1 red bell pepper, cut into strips
1 onion, thinly sliced
1 (10-ounce) can chopped tomatoes with green chiles
1 (8-ounce) can tomato sauce
2 tablespoons honey
2 Granny Smith apples, cut into 1-inch pieces
1 (15-ounce) can dark red kidney beans
2 tablespoons chopped fresh parsley

Combine the flour, cumin, chili powder, garlic powder and cinnamon in a large bowl. Add the beef cubes and toss to coat well. Heat the oil in a large skillet. Brown the beef cubes on all sides in the skillet. Spoon into a large stockpot. Add the beef broth and apple juice. Simmer, covered, over medium heat for 1 hour or until the beef cubes are cooked through and tender.

Add the potatoes, bell peppers, onion, tomatoes with green chiles, tomato sauce and honey. Simmer, covered, for 35 minutes or until the potatoes are tender. Add the apples and kidney beans. Simmer, covered, for 15 minutes or until the apples are tender. Stir in the parsley. Ladle into bowls to serve. You may garnish with shredded Cheddar cheese and chopped black olives if desired.

Serves 6

Steak Diane

1 tablespoon butter
2 tablespoons finely chopped shallots
2 garlic cloves, minced
1 cup sliced fresh mushrooms
4 boneless rib-eye steaks or New York strip steaks
1/2 cup beef broth
2 teaspoons Dijon mustard
1 teaspoon Worcestershire sauce
2 tablespoons brandy

Melt the butter in a large skillet over medium heat. Add the shallots and garlic and sauté for 2 minutes. Stir in the mushrooms and sauté for 4 minutes. Remove the shallots, garlic and mushrooms with a slotted spoon to a bowl. Increase the heat to medium-high. Add the steaks to the skillet. Cook for 6 to 7 minutes for medium-rare, turning once. Cook longer for the desired degree of doneness. Remove to a platter and keep warm. Decrease the heat to medium.

Add the broth, Dijon mustard, Worcestershire sauce and the reserved mushroom mixture. Bring to a boil and cook until the sauce is slightly reduced, stirring constantly. Heat the brandy in a small saucepan. Ignite with a match and pour the flaming brandy over the sauce. Spoon the sauce over the steaks. Serve immediately.

Serves 4

Cider-Braised Pork Roast

2 tablespoons vegetable oil
1 1/2 to 2 pounds boneless pork roast, trimmed
1 1/4 cups apple cider or juice
1 onion, chopped
1/2 teaspoon salt
2 Granny Smith apples, cut into wedges
1 (6-ounce) package dried apricot halves
1/2 teaspoon cardamom
1/4 teaspoon cinnamon

Heat the oil in a Dutch oven. Brown the roast in the hot oil on all sides; drain. Add the apple cider, onion and salt; bring to a boil. Reduce the heat and simmer, covered, for 45 minutes. Add the apples, apricots, cardamom and cinnamon; bring to a boil. Reduce the heat and simmer, covered, for 10 minutes or until the pork is tender and a meat thermometer registers 160 degrees.

Remove the roast and fruit with a slotted spoon to a serving platter and keep warm. Bring the remaining sauce to a boil and cook for 5 to 10 minutes or until reduced to 1/2 cup. Spoon over the roast and fruit. Garnish with fresh thyme sprigs.

Serves 6

Country Pork with Apple Kraut

Combined with new potatoes and pickled beets, this makes a warm and filling winter meal.

1 tablespoon vegetable oil
2 pounds country-style pork ribs
1 onion, chopped
1 (14-ounce) can sauerkraut
1 cup applesauce
2 tablespoons brown sugar
2 teaspoons caraway seeds
1 teaspoon garlic powder
1/2 teaspoon pepper

Heat the oil in a Dutch oven. Add the ribs and onion. Cook until the ribs are browned on all sides and the onion is tender. Remove from the heat. Combine the sauerkraut, applesauce, brown sugar, caraway seeds, garlic powder and pepper in a bowl and mix well. Pour over the ribs. Bake, covered, at 350 degrees for 1 1/2 to 2 hours or until the ribs are tender.

Serves 4

Hawaiian Chicken and Pears

This easy one-dish meal combines vegetables, pears, and pineapple with chicken.

- 1 pound chicken breasts, thinly sliced
- 3 tablespoons butter or margarine
- 1 (8-ounce) can pineapple chunks
- 4 Anjou pears, sliced
- 1/2 green bell pepper, sliced
- 1/2 cup cashews
- 2 tablespoons brown sugar
- 1 tablespoon cornstarch
- 1/3 cup water
- 2 tablespoons soy sauce

Sauté the chicken in the butter in a skillet for 3 to 5 minutes or until the juices run clear when pierced with a fork. Drain the pineapple, reserving 1/3 cup of the juice. Add the pineapple, pears, bell pepper and cashews to the skillet. Cook until heated through. Combine the brown sugar, cornstarch, reserved pineapple juice, water and soy sauce in a saucepan. Cook over low heat until the mixture thickens, stirring constantly. Cook for 1 minute longer. Pour the sauce over the chicken mixture and mix gently. Serve over hot cooked rice.

Serves 4 to 6

Weekend Chicken Chili

1 pound Great Northern beans
2 pounds boneless chicken breasts
3 1/2 cups water
1 tablespoon olive oil
2 onions, finely chopped
4 garlic cloves, minced
2 (4-ounce) cans diced green chiles, drained
2 teaspoons cumin
1 1/2 teaspoons oregano
1/4 teaspoon ground cloves
1/4 teaspoon cayenne pepper
6 cups canned chicken broth
Salt to taste
2 cups (8 ounces) shredded Monterey Jack cheese
Sour cream
Salsa
Diced tomatoes
Chopped green onions
Chopped fresh cilantro

Soak the beans in enough water to cover in a large heavy stockpot for 8 hours. Combine the chicken and water in a large stockpot. Bring to a boil, reduce the heat and simmer, covered, for 30 minutes. Remove the chicken and cool. Shred the chicken into bite-size pieces. Rinse the beans; drain and set aside. Heat the olive oil in a large heavy stockpot. Sauté the onions in the heated olive oil for 10 minutes. Add the garlic, green chiles, cumin, oregano, cloves and cayenne pepper. Cook for a few minutes longer.

Add the broth and beans and cook for 2 hours or until the beans are tender. Stir in the chicken and salt; cook until heated through. Stir in the cheese gradually. Cook until the cheese melts; do not bring to a boil. Ladle into bowls to serve. Top with any or all of the following: sour cream, salsa, diced tomatoes, chopped green onions or chopped fresh cilantro. Serve with your favorite corn bread.

Serves 6

Chicken and Caramelized Onion Pizza

This is a great dinner to make with the whole family. Kids love to help assemble the pizza. Serve with a green salad.

2 tablespoons butter
1 large Walla Walla onion, thinly sliced
1 boneless skinless chicken breast
Barbecue sauce
1 loaf frozen bread dough, thawed
1 tablespoon olive oil
2 tablespoons roasted salted cashew nuts
1/4 cup grated asiago cheese
1/4 cup grated Parmesan cheese
4 ounces fresh mozzarella cheese

Heat the butter in a skillet. Sauté the onion slices until caramelized; set aside. Brush the chicken breast with barbecue sauce. Grill or broil the chicken for 15 to 20 minutes or until cooked through and the juices run clear when pierced with a fork. Slice the chicken into thin strips; set aside. Roll out the bread dough into a large circle 1/4 inch thick. Brush the dough with the olive oil, adding more if necessary to coat evenly. Place the dough on a baking sheet or pizza stone.

Arrange the cashews and chicken strips over the dough. Arrange the caramelized onions over the top. Sprinkle with the asiago cheese and Parmesan cheese. Tear the mozzarella cheese into small pieces and arrange over the top. Bake at 425 degrees for 15 minutes or until the cheese is bubbly and the crust is golden brown.

Serves 4 to 6

Tortellini with Gorgonzola Sauce

8 ounces tortellini, cooked
2 tablespoons light Italian vinaigrette dressing
3 ounces gorgonzola cheese, crumbled
1/4 cup milk
1/2 cup sour cream
1 garlic clove, minced
1 teaspoon fresh lemon juice
1/4 teaspoon salt
1/2 cup chopped toasted walnuts

Toss the cooked tortellini with the vinaigrette in a large bowl. Chill until serving time.

Combine the cheese, milk, sour cream, garlic, lemon juice and salt in a bowl and mix well. Stir the walnuts into the sauce immediately before serving. Pour into a serving bowl. Serve the tortellini on the side.

Serves 6

Winter Farm Breakfast

Start your day the Yakima way with this hearty breakfast.

1 pound bacon, chopped
1 onion, chopped
1 (32-ounce) package frozen shredded hash brown potatoes, thawed
10 eggs
Salt to taste
Pepper to taste
2 cups (8 ounces) shredded Cheddar cheese
1/4 cup chopped fresh parsley

Cook the bacon and onion in a large skillet until the bacon is tender-crisp. Drain, reserving 1/2 cup of the drippings in the skillet. Add the potatoes to the skillet and mix well. Cook over medium heat for 10 minutes or until the potatoes are brown. Make 10 small wells in the potato mixture. Crack 1 egg into each well. Sprinkle with salt and pepper. Cook, covered, over low heat for 10 minutes or until the eggs are cooked to the desired degree of doneness. Sprinkle with the cheese. Cook for 2 minutes longer or until the cheese is melted. Sprinkle with the parsley. Serve immediately.

Note: You may top the cheese with sliced tomatoes if desired. To spice it up, add chopped green and red bell peppers, chopped tomatoes and 1 small can chopped green chiles.

Serves 4 to 6

Apple Cranberry Nut Bread

1 cup fresh cranberries, chopped
2 cups applesauce
4 cups sifted flour
2 cups sugar
4 teaspoons baking powder
2 teaspoons baking soda
1 teaspoon salt
1 1/2 cups chopped pecans
2 eggs, beaten
2/3 cup orange juice
6 tablespoons melted butter

Combine the cranberries and applesauce in a small bowl; set aside. Combine the flour, sugar, baking powder, baking soda and salt in a bowl and mix well. Add the applesauce mixture and pecans and mix well. Add the eggs, orange juice and melted butter and mix well. Pour into 2 large loaf pans or 4 small loaf pans. Bake at 350 degrees for 50 to 60 minutes for large pans or 40 minutes for the small pans or until a wooden pick inserted in the center comes out clean.

Makes 2 large loaves or 4 small loaves

Fresh Pear Bread

1/2 cup (1 stick) butter, softened
1 cup sugar
2 eggs
2 cups flour
1/2 teaspoon salt
1/2 teaspoon baking soda
1/8 teaspoon nutmeg
1/4 cup plain yogurt or buttermilk
1 cup coarsely chopped pear
1 teaspoon vanilla extract

Beat the butter and sugar in a mixing bowl until light and creamy. Beat in the eggs 1 at a time, beating well after each addition. Combine the flour, salt, baking soda and nutmeg in a bowl. Beat in the flour mixture alternately with the yogurt. Stir in the pears and vanilla. Pour into a 5×9-inch loaf pan. Bake at 350 degrees for 1 hour.

Makes 1 large loaf

Carrot Cake with Cream Cheese Frosting

CAKE
2 cups flour
2 teaspoons baking soda
2 teaspoons cinnamon
1/2 teaspoon ginger
1/2 teaspoon salt
3 eggs
1 1/2 cups sugar
3/4 cup mayonnaise
1 (8-ounce) can crushed pineapple, drained
2 cups coarsely grated carrots
3/4 cup coarsely chopped walnuts (optional)

CREAM CHEESE FROSTING
1 cup (2 sticks) butter, softened
16 ounces cream cheese, softened
2 teaspoons vanilla extract
2 (1-pound) packages confectioners' sugar

For the cake, combine the flour, baking soda, cinnamon, ginger and salt in a bowl. Beat the eggs, sugar and mayonnaise in a mixing bowl until well blended. Beat in the pineapple. Stir in the carrots and walnuts. Pour into 2 greased and floured 9-inch cake pans.

Bake at 350 degrees for 30 to 35 minutes or until a cake tester inserted in the center comes out clean. Cool in the pans for 10 minutes. Invert the layers on a wire rack to cool completely.

For the frosting, beat the butter and cream cheese in a mixing bowl until light and creamy. Beat in the vanilla. Add the confectioners' sugar gradually, beating constantly until smooth. Spread the frosting between the layers and over the top and side of the cake.

Serves 12

Fudge Cake with Chocolate Rum Glaze

CAKE

- 3/4 cup plus 2 tablespoons cake flour
- 1 teaspoon baking powder
- 1/2 teaspoon baking soda
- 1/2 teaspoon salt
- 2 ounces unsweetened baking chocolate, broken into pieces
- 1 1/4 cups sugar
- 1 tablespoon baking cocoa
- 1/3 cup boiling water
- 2 large eggs
- 3/4 cup (1 1/2 sticks) unsalted butter, cut into 6 pats and softened
- 1/2 cup sour cream
- 1 tablespoon dark rum

GLAZE

- 3 ounces sweet chocolate
- 2 tablespoons water
- 2 tablespoons unsalted butter
- 1/4 cup confectioners' sugar
- Pinch of salt
- 1 teaspoon dark rum

For the cake, cut a round piece of parchment paper to fit the bottom of an 8-inch springform pan. Place it in the bottom of the pan. Butter the paper and side of the pan. Combine the cake flour, baking powder, baking soda and salt in a food processor. Process for 5 seconds to mix well. Pour into a bowl and set aside. Combine the chocolate, 1/4 cup of the sugar and baking cocoa in the processor. Process for 1 minute or until the chocolate is finely minced. Add the boiling water in a fine stream, processing until the chocolate is melted. Add the eggs and process for 1 minute. Add the remaining sugar and process for 1 minute, stopping once to scrape down the bowl. Add the butter and process for 1 minute. Add the sour cream and rum and process for 5 seconds. Add the flour mixture and pulse 3 or 4 times or just until flour is blended. Pour the batter into the prepared pan, spreading evenly with a spatula. Bake at 325 degrees for 50 to 55 minutes or until the cake begins to pull away from the side of the pan. Let the cake cool in the pan on a wire rack. Place on a serving plate and remove the side from the pan.

For the glaze, combine the chocolate, water, butter and confectioners' sugar in the top of a double boiler. Cook over low heat until the chocolate is melted and the mixture is heated through. Stir in the rum. Pour into a bowl. Chill until the glaze has thickened. Spread the glaze over the top and side of the cake with a spatula.

Serves 10

Cranberry and Pear Crisp

2 pears, peeled and sliced
2 tablespoons dried cranberries
1 tablespoon brown sugar
1 tablespoon whole wheat flour
1/4 teaspoon cinnamon
1/2 teaspoon ginger
1/4 teaspoon vanilla extract
3 tablespoons brown sugar
2 tablespoons whole wheat flour
2 tablespoons rolled oats
1 tablespoon sliced almonds
1/4 teaspoon cinnamon
2 teaspoons butter

Combine the pears, cranberries, 1 tablespoon brown sugar, 1 tablespoon whole wheat flour, 1/4 teaspoon cinnamon, ginger and vanilla in a small bowl and mix well. Spoon into a greased 2-cup oval baking dish. Combine 3 tablespoons brown sugar, 2 tablespoons whole wheat flour, oats, almonds and 1/4 teaspoon cinnamon in a small bowl and mix well. Cut in the butter until crumbly. Sprinkle over the pear mixture. Bake at 375 degrees for 25 minutes or until bubbly and the topping is golden brown. Serve warm with vanilla ice cream or frozen yogurt. Sprinkle cinnamon over the top.

Serves 4

Start with fresh coffee beans and grind as necessary to maintain the ultimate in fresh flavor. Store coffee beans in an airtight container away from air, heat, light, and moisture. You may also store your coffee beans in the freezer, but let them defrost prior to grinding so that there is not moisture in the grounds. Always brew coffee with clean, cold filtered water for a crisper, cleaner taste. For ICED COFFEE, brew double the amount of coffee grounds to the amount of water. Add ice and chill until cold.

Country Pear Tart

TART PASTRY
1 2/3 cups flour
1/4 teaspoon salt
1/2 cup (1 stick) chilled unsalted butter, cut into pats
1/4 cup sugar
2 egg yolks
2 tablespoons (or more) ice water
3 tablespoons apricot jam

FILLING
1/2 cup dried tart cherries
1/4 cup brandy or apple juice
1/4 cup sugar
2 tablespoons cornstarch
1/4 teaspoon cinnamon
4 cups sliced peeled pears
1 teaspoon lemon zest
1 teaspoon vanilla extract
1 tablespoon sliced almonds

For the pastry, combine the flour and salt in a food processor. Add the butter and pulse until the mixture is crumbly. Add the sugar and egg yolks and process until blended. Add the water and process until the mixture is moist and clumps begin to form. Add more water if mixture is too dry. Shape the dough into a ball and flatten into a disk. Wrap in plastic wrap and chill for 30 minutes or until the dough is firm. Roll the dough out into a 12-inch circle on a floured surface. Arrange in a 9-inch tart pan with a removable bottom. Trim crust to 1/4 inch; fold in. Freeze for 15 minutes. Line the crust with foil; fill with dried beans or pie weights. Bake at 350 degrees for 20 minutes. Remove the foil and beans; bake 15 minutes longer. Brush with jam; bake 5 minutes longer.

For the filling, combine the cherries and brandy in a small saucepan. Heat over low heat until the mixture is hot, but not boiling. Remove from the heat. Let stand. Combine the sugar, cornstarch and cinnamon in a large bowl. Stir in the pears, cherry mixture, lemon zest and vanilla. Spoon the mixture into the center of the pastry. Sprinkle with almonds. Bake at 375 degrees for 40 to 45 minutes or until the crust is golden brown. Cool for 30 minutes before serving.

Serves 10

Pear and Walnut Bars

1 3/4 cups flour
3/4 cup confectioners' sugar
3/4 cup (1 1/4 sticks) butter, softened
1/2 teaspoon cinnamon
1/2 cup chopped walnuts
3 ripe Bartlett pears, peeled and sliced
2 eggs
1/3 cup packed brown sugar
1 1/2 teaspoons vanilla extract
1/2 teaspoon cinnamon

Combine the flour, confectioners' sugar, butter and 1/2 teaspoon cinnamon in a bowl and mix well. Press into the bottom of a greased 7×11-inch baking dish. Sprinkle the walnuts over the bottom. Layer the pear slices evenly over the walnuts. Beat the eggs, brown sugar, vanilla and 1/2 teaspoon cinnamon in a bowl until well blended. Pour over the pears. Bake at 350 degrees for 35 to 40 minutes or until golden brown. Cool before cutting into bars to serve.

Makes 12 bars

Oatmeal Pear Cookies

1/2 cup (1 stick) butter, softened
1 cup packed brown sugar
1 egg
2 cups rolled oats
1 1/2 cups flour
2 ripe Bartlett pears, coarsely chopped
1 1/4 teaspoons cinnamon
1 teaspoon vanilla extract
1/2 teaspoon baking soda
1/2 teaspoon salt

Beat the butter and brown sugar in a mixing bowl until light and creamy. Beat in the egg, oats, flour, pears, cinnamon, vanilla, baking soda and salt. Drop by rounded teaspoons onto a lightly greased cookie sheet. Sprinkle the tops generously with granulated sugar if desired. Bake at 350 degrees for 15 minutes or until light brown

Makes 4 dozen cookies

Orange-Glazed Pear Bars

BARS
3 cups flour
1 1/2 teaspoons salt
1 cup shortening
1/2 cup milk
1/2 cup fine bread crumbs
6 ripe Bartlett pears, peeled and sliced
1/2 cup sugar
1 teaspoon orange zest
Milk

ORANGE GLAZE
1 cup sifted confectioners' sugar
2 tablespoons orange juice
3/4 teaspoon vanilla extract

FOR THE BARS, combine the flour and salt in a bowl. Cut in the shortening until crumbly. Stir in the milk 1 tablespoon at a time until moistened. Divide the dough into halves. Roll out 1/2 of the dough into a 12×17-inch rectangle. Place in a 10×15-inch jelly roll pan. Sprinkle with the bread crumbs. Arrange the pear slices in the bottom. Combine the sugar and orange zest in a small bowl; sprinkle over the pear slices. Roll out the remaining dough to a 10×15-inch rectangle and place on top of the pears. Seal and flute the edges. Cut several steam vents in the top. Brush the top of the pastry with milk. Bake at 375 degrees for 45 to 55 minutes or until the pastry is golden brown. Brush with the Orange Glaze while warm. Cool before cutting into bars to serve.

FOR THE GLAZE, combine the confectioners' sugar, orange juice and vanilla in a small bowl.

Makes 3 to 4 dozen bars

NORTHWEST PEARS

The Pacific Northwest (the states of Oregon and Washington) is home to some of the nation's most productive farmland. To grow the best pears, an optimum combination of soil, moisture, and climate conditions must be present. In the Northwest, where 90 percent of the nation's fresh winter pears are grown, conditions are perfect. According to Native American legend, the word "Yakama" means "Black Bear." Each year the plentiful water and rich, light, fertile soil of the beautiful Yakima Valley bring thousands of acres of Northwest Pear trees into bloom.

YELLOW BARTLETT
August–January. Ripens to a bright yellow Aromatic and perfect for fresh eating Sweet and juicy and excellent for canning and cooking

RED BARTLETT
August–January. Bright red skin when fully ripe Same flavor, texture, and use as the yellow Bartlett

GREEN ANJOU
October–June. Abundant juice and sweet flavor when ripe Do not change color when ripe

RED ANJOU
October–May. Same flavor and texture as green Anjou Remains maroon red when ripe

BOSC
August–April. Highly aromatic and flavorful pear Dense flesh makes ideal for baking and cooking Brown and russeted color

COMICE
August–February. One of the sweetest and juiciest varieties, and often very large An elegant dessert pear; excellent served as a dessert with cheese course

SECKEL
August–February. Tiny pears with an ultra-sweet flavor Excellent choice for children's snack, pickling, or as a garnish

Washington Apples

The fertile valleys and plateaus of America's Far West produce the world's best apples. More than 225,000 acres of apple orchards are nestled in the eastern foothills of the picturesque Cascade Mountains at elevations from 500 to 3,000 feet above sea level. The orchards are irrigated with plentiful and cool mountain water.

This fertile area first became known to American pioneers at the turn of the nineteenth century. By 1826, early settlers had discovered the area's rich lava-ash soil, and plentiful sunshine created perfect conditions for growing apples. The arid climate also meant fewer insect and disease problems, while producing an apple with a smoother finish than those in some other growing areas.

Noting the health and vigor of apple trees planted along stream banks, pioneers developed irrigation systems and, by 1889, commercial orchards were established. Most apple-growing districts in Washington state are still located along the banks of major rivers.

The average size of an orchard is about 100 acres, but some cover as many as 3,000 acres and employ 300 or more workers year-round. An estimated 35,000 to 45,000 pickers are employed during the peak of harvest.

Washington state growers successfully harvest a wide variety of apples, including Red and Golden Delicious, Granny Smith, Braeburn, Jonagold, Fuji, Gala, and many others. Orchardists continually improve growing methods to produce apples that are crisper, juicier, more flavorful, and store better.

- More than half of all apples grown in the United States for fresh eating come from orchards in Washington state.
- One apple has 5 grams of fiber, supplying 20 percent of the daily fiber recommendation.
- Washington apples are sold in all 50 states and in more than 40 countries.
- Americans eat approximately 19.6 pounds of fresh apples annually, as compared to about 46 pounds consumed annually by residents of European countries.

Washington Apple Varieties

BRAEBURN
Tart-sweet and hard crisp; very good in pies; good in fresh salads and sauces; and for baking and freezing; in season October through July

CAMEO®
Sweet and crisp; excellent in fresh salads, pies, and sauces and for baking; very good for freezing; in season October through August

FUJI
Sweet-tart and hard crisp; excellent in fresh salads; good in pies and sauces and for baking and freezing; in season year-round

GALA
Very sweet and delicate crisp; very good in fresh salads and sauces; good in pies and for baking and freezing; in season August through March

GOLDEN DELICIOUS
Sweet and delicate crisp; excellent in pies; very good for baking and freezing and in fresh salads and sauces; in season year-round

GRANNY SMITH
Tart and hard crisp; very good in fresh salads, pies, and sauces and for baking and freezing; in season year-round

JONAGOLD
Sweet-tart and delicate crisp; excellent in pies; very good in fresh salads and for baking and freezing; good in sauces; in season September through April

PINK LADY®
Tart-sweet and hard crisp; excellent in fresh salads and pies; very good in sauces and for freezing; good for baking; in season October through June

RED DELICIOUS
Sweet and crisp; excellent for fresh salads; fair in pies and sauces and for freezing; not recommended for baking; in season year-round

Homemade Caramel Apples

1 (14-ounce) bag caramel candies, unwrapped
2 tablespoons water
Washington Red Delicious apples
Wooden sticks

Combine the unwrapped caramel squares and water in a microwave-safe bowl. Microwave on High for 3 to 4 minutes or until the caramels are melted. Stir once or twice. You may also melt the caramels in a saucepan over low heat, stirring constantly to prevent sticking.

Rinse and dry the apples. Insert the wooden sticks firmly in the top of the apples. Wipe away any juice on the apple to ensure the apples are completely dry. Dip the apples in the melted caramel and place on waxed paper on a baking sheet to set. You may roll the apples in assorted toppings such as chopped nuts or chocolate candy sprinkles. Refrigerate until serving time to keep the caramel firm.

Makes variable

Hot Apple Tea

6 cups Washington apple juice or cider
3 tablespoons lemon juice
1/2 cup packed brown sugar
1 cinnamon stick
1 teaspoon whole cloves
1/2 teaspoon whole allspice
2 tea bags

Combine the apple juice, lemon juice, brown sugar, cinnamon stick, cloves and allspice in a 3-quart saucepan. Cook over medium heat until the mixture begins to boil. Reduce the heat and simmer for 5 minutes. Remove from the heat and add the tea bags. Let steep for 5 minutes. Strain to remove the spices and tea bags. Serve hot.

Serves 8

Apple Butter

4 pounds Granny Smith apples, peeled and quartered
1 cup water
1 cup apple cider
Brown sugar
2 teaspoons cinnamon
1 teaspoon ground cloves
1/2 teaspoon allspice
Grated zest and juice of 2 lemons

Combine the apples, water and apple cider in a large stockpot. Cook over medium heat until the apples are very soft. Purée the apples in a food mill. Add 1/2 cup brown sugar for each cup of apple purée and mix well in a large stockpot. Stir in the cinnamon, cloves, allspice, lemon zest and lemon juice. Cook over low heat for 3 to 4 hours or until thick and dark brown. You may also cook in a slow cooker. If not used within 2 weeks, pour into hot sterilized jars and seal tightly.

Makes 5 pints

Old-Fashioned Applesauce

8 pounds Granny Smith apples
1/2 cup water
Sugar to taste
Cinnamon to taste

Core and quarter the apples. Place the apples in a large heavy stockpot with a tight-fitting lid. Add the water. Cook over low heat until the apples are very soft. Purée in a food mill. Spoon into a serving bowl. Stir in sugar and cinnamon. Serve immediately or store in the refrigerator.

Makes 2 quarts

All About Cider

When the Romans arrived in England in 55 B.C., they were reported to have found the local Kentish villagers drinking a cider-like beverage made from apples. By the beginning of the ninth century, cider drinking was well established in Europe and a reference recorded by Charlemagne clearly confirms its popularity. During medieval times, cider making was an important industry. Monasteries sold vast quantities of their strong, spiced cider to the public. English cider making probably peaked around the mid-seventeenth century, when almost every farm had its own cider orchard and press.

Early English settlers introduced cider to America by bringing with them the seeds for growing cider apples. During the colonial period, hard cider was one of America's most popular beverages. Today, traditional cider making is enjoying a resurgence in popularity in both America and Europe.

Most cider is made from fermented apple juice. Natural cider has nothing added and relies on the wild yeast present in the apples for fermentation. For mass-produced ciders, a yeast culture is added in order to achieve consistency. Although much of today's cider is produced from apple concentrate, many traditional cider makers use only cider apples, cultivated specifically for the purpose of cider making.

Both traditional and mass-market ciders are available carbonated or still and range in style from the very dry to the extremely sweet. In Europe, "cider" refers to fermented apple juice that contains varying levels of alcohol. In the United States, fermented apple juice is known as "hard cider," and unfermented, freshly expressed juice is called "sweet cider."

Sparkling Cider

2 1/2 cups orange juice
1 1/2 cups tangerine juice
1 bottle sparkling apple cider, chilled
1/4 cup grenadine

Strain the orange and tangerine juices through a cheesecloth-lined colander into a large bowl, discarding the pulp. Combine the juices and cider in a large pitcher; mix well. Pour 3/4 cup into 8 old-fashioned glasses. Pour 1 1/2 teaspoons grenadine into each glass slowly; do not stir. Serve immediately.

Serves 8

Hot Apple Raspberry Cider

8 cups Washington apple cider or apple juice
1 cup frozen raspberry juice concentrate, thawed
1/4 cup sugar
1 cinnamon stick

Combine the cider, raspberry juice concentrate, sugar and cinnamon stick in a 4-quart saucepan. Cook over medium heat until the mixture begins to boil, stirring occasionally. Reduce the heat and simmer for 10 minutes. Remove from the heat. Remove the cinnamon stick. Serve hot.

Serves 8

Herbs and Spices

BASIL
Clove-like taste, sweet; different varieties; essential for Italian cooking; good with eggs, pasta, tomatoes, fish, chicken, and shellfish

CARDAMOM
Cinnamon-like seed; popular in Indian food, baking, spice cakes, cookies, apple/pumpkin pies, curries, squash, and sweet potatoes

CHIVES
Light onion taste; good in cream soups, sauces, fish, shellfish, and eggs

CILANTRO
Lively, pungent; essential in Mexican, Latin American, and Asian cooking; use in rice, beans, fish, shellfish, poultry, vegetables, salsas, and salads; add fresh just before serving

CINNAMON
Sweet, hot flavor; use in spice cakes, cookies, fruit, squash, custards, carrots, and sweet potatoes

CLOVES
Pungent and sweet; use to flavor stocks, ham, spice cakes, cookies, breads, pies, sauces, sweet potatoes, squash, and carrots

DILL
Delicate caraway taste; use for pickles; use seeds with rice and fish; use fresh dill with eggs, cheese, yogurt, seafood, chicken, cucumbers, green beans, potatoes, tomatoes, and beets

GINGER

Versatile spice with bite and aroma; popular in Jamaican and German cuisines; use dried ginger in cakes, cookies, fruit, pies, custards, rice, and marinades; use crystallized ginger in cakes, cookies, tea, or as a snack; use fresh gingerroot sliced and grated in marinades with fish, poultry, pork, and vegetables

LAVENDER

Fresh clean scent; good added to fruit and iced tea

LEMON GRASS

Woodsy, lemon flavor; popular in Indonesian and Near Eastern cooking; use with fish, shellfish, chicken soup, salsa, and vinaigrettes; low heat brings out flavor

MINT

Refreshing scent and cool taste; thirty varieties—spearmint and peppermint are the best known; popular in Middle Eastern yogurt and grain dishes and in salads; use with peas, beans, corn, potatoes, jellies, fruit salads, desserts, and iced tea

NUTMEG

Sweet, nutty spice; size of an olive; best in cream sauces, soups, beans, broccoli, carrots, cauliflower, spinach, onions, cakes, cookies, pies, pastries, and eggnog; ground nutmeg loses its flavor quickly; buy whole; grate as needed

OREGANO

Pungent marjoram taste (delicate taste); use with meat, fish, poultry, beans, cheese, eggs, vegetables, tomatoes, and eggplant; known in Italian, Greek, and Mexican cooking

Wines and Cheeses

Wines of the same variety can differ in flavor just like cheeses, so nothing is absolute; take the following as mere suggestions:

BRIE
Cabernet sauvignon, Champagne, pinot noir, cabernet franc,Washington Syrah

CHEDDAR (EXTRA-SHARP)
Port, cabernet sauvignon, Syrah, gewürztraminer

CHÈVRE (FRESH)
Merlot, cabernet sauvignon, pinot noir, sauvignon blanc, gewürztraminer

EDAM
Champagne, late-harvest wines, dry chenin blanc

FETA
Sauvignon blanc, Champagne, late-harvest wines

GOUDA (AGED)
Chardonnay, port, riesling, later-harvest wines, sauvignon blanc

MONTEREY JACK
Dry rosé, gamay beaujolais rosé

MOZZARELLA
Many reds, gamay beaujolais rosé

ROQUEFORT
Some cabernet sauvignons, late-harvest Semillon or riesling, brut Champagne

SWISS
Chardonnay, riesling, chenin blanc, sauvignon blanc, dry rosé

The committee of FRESH FROM THE VALLEY would like to thank the following sponsors for their generous financial support:

COVER SPONSOR

YAKIMA VALLEY
MEMORIAL
AWARD WINNING HOSPITAL

CHAPTER SPONSORS

Jackie Velikanje
Janet LeCocq
Sharon Smith
Marie Halverson
Sally Douglas
Nancy Rossmeissl
Okie Applegate
LeeAnn Hughes

COMMUNITY SPONSORS

Birchfield Manor
Gasperetti's
Inaba Farms
Inland Fruit & Produce, Inc.
Menke, Jackson, Beyer, Elofson, Ehlis & Harper LLP
Noel Corporation
Prediletto, Halpin, Scharnikow & Nelson, PS
Dr. Jeffrey Pruiett, D.M.D.
Terrill, Lewis & Wilke Insurance, Inc.

Contributors

We would also like to thank the following inividuals and their families for sharing their favorite recipes and volunteering to test new recipes, and we extend a special thank you to artist Felicia Holtzinger for her artwork used in the book.

Lisette Allan*
Martha Barringer
Jennifer Bliesner
Mary-beth Bradley
Linda Brestar
Hilary Brooks
Patricia Busse
Debbie Cameron
Kay Carberry
Diane Carey
Kris Carlson
Cathleen Carpenter
Nicole Colgan
Janine Connell
Kelly Connelly
Amy Conrad*
Kathryn Culpepper
Gail Davis
Carol-Anne De La Chapelle
Amy Dodge
Sally Douglas
Linda Drumhiller
Anna Marie Dufault
Bobbie Dwinell
Marcie Ehlis*
Sandy Engquist
Connie Farina
Helen Faringer*
Julie Farrow
JoAnn Funk
Pat Gates
Lori Gibbons
Ellen Gibson
Lynn Gilmore
Marie Halverson
Cherie Hanses
Terri Hanses*
Cindy Hargreaves
Janette Heinbaugh
Karen Hefner
Ginger Hislop
Tanya Hoff*
Merrilee Hurson
Kitty Inaba
Shana Irby*
Karen Johnson
Tahni Kalina
Lynn Katz
Stacy Kellogg
Karin Kerns
Kim Kershaw
Jennifer King
Joan LaFramboise
Janet LeCocq
Rhea Lewis
Linda Linneweh
Lisa Long
Kim Loranz*
Chris Losee
Traci Lust
Leslie Mahoney
Ericka Masset
Elizabeth McGree
Amy McKinney
Eileen Merrell
Margaret Morris
Rebecca Munson
Diane Murphy
Amy Neal
Mackie Neumann
Carrie Nyssen
Kathy O'Meara-Wyman
Meg Brooks Pehlke
Sandra Peterson
Darlene Picatti
Lisa Plath
Karen Pratt
Trina Price
Patty Pruitt*
Jackie Ray
Ericka Reiber*
Walt Reiber
Amy Richardson
Jean Rothenbueler
Sunny Rowland*
Ellen Roy
Kim Shields
Sharon Smith
Jenny Snyder
Mary Lee Splawn
Heidi Stevens*
Sue Stevenson
Pam Tabert*
TJ Tjarnberg
Julie Toney
Lisa Wallace
Diana Wallin
Dorothy Wolf

*Fresh from the Valley Committee Member

Index

Sources:
Pear Bureau Northwest—www.usapears.com
Washington State Apple Commission—www.bestapples.com
Washington State University Creamery—www.wsu.edu/creamery

FRESH FROM THE VALLEY

A Harvest of Recipes from the
Junior League of Yakima
5000 West Lincoln Avenue
Yakima, Washington 98908
509-966-0930

YOUR ORDER	QTY	TOTAL
FRESH FROM THE VALLEY at $19.95 each		$
Washington residents add 7.9% sales tax		$
Postage and handling at $3.00 each		$
	TOTAL	$

Name

Street Address

City State Zip

Telephone

Please make check payable to Junior League of Yakima.

Photocopies will be accepted.